# On The Trail Of Lyman Dillon

**By Douglas Monk**

2016 Orchard Press

# Acknowledgements

There are several people I want to thank as this goes to print;

First, my wife Micaela, for her whole hearted support from the very beginning on this project.

Joy Adams, for the hours and hours of time we spent making road trips, taking pictures, etc.

Evan Vulich from E&L Graphics for the hours of work he put into cover design, photo editing, and layout of the book manuscript.

Steve Hanken, for the hours of conversations we spent discussing local history.

Kristina "Lucy" Pasquan, for helping me line up two editors for my rough draft...Tracy Griffis and Allison Jensen, both from Washington State.

Pam Foley, for sharing her dad's research material with me.

Bill and Jane Corbin, for opening their home to me and being willing to share some of his wealth of knowledge on local history.

Archaeologist, Cindy Peterson, for going with us to the *Iowa Historical Society* archive library.

Larry and Kathy Pisarik, for lining up several of the host families while on my walk, including Ron and Mary Holubar from Solon, Dorothy Rilett from Mount Vernon, Casey and Christina Ditch from Anamosa, and Mr. and Mrs. James Schuester from Cascade.

Becky Dirks Haugsted from the *Anamosa Newspaper*, for putting together a DVD of my walk.

I want to thank Richard Eugene Stimmel and his dad, Richard Gene Stimmel, from Maquoketa, Iowa, for reaching out to me last winter. Richard Gene Stimmel was interested in Lyman Dillon because he was a direct descendant of the Rohret boys who helped Dillon with the supply wagon and direct the oxen as they plowed.

Finally, I want to thank those of you that helped financially get this book to print.

Sincerely, Douglas Monk ©2016

# Table of Contents

## Chapter 1 • Iowa City to Solon  1

- September 8, 2008
- Iowa City
- Chauncey Swan
- Phillip Clark

## Chapter 2 • Solon To Mount Vernon  10

- September 9, 2008
- The White Wolf
- Horse Thieves (Brody Family)

## Chapter 3 • Mount Vernon to Anamosa  16

- September 10, 2008
- Reception at Martelle
- Stopping by The Anamosa Eureka
- Edmund Booth

## Chapter 4 • Anamosa to Monticello  28

- September 11, 2008
- John Lovejoy
- Scotch Grove's First Settlers From the Red River Valley
- Langworthy - Wade Family Tragedy
- Stories About Grandpa Monk and Marie Otten

## Chapter 5 • Monticello to North of Cascade   42

## Chapter 6 • Cascade to Dubuque   51

## Chapter 7 • Gus Norlin's Research  73

Note: Gus used to be the president of *The Jones County Historical Society.* One of his ongoing interests and projects had been researching Lyman Dillon and Dillon's Furrow. Pam Foley, Gus's daughter, shared with me his notes, newspaper clippings, and original correspondence after he passed away. I am including a previously unpublished paper he wrote in this book as one more way to keep the local history of our area alive for future generations.

# Introduction

*"I can still see that man... had a damn rod as thick as my arm over his arm... he was laying there, couldn't move. Both engines were lying in the ditch. Then the doctor hollered; "Does anybody got some whiskey??? Come on, get some! If you got nothing, get some! We've got to have whiskey for this guy." They poured the whole pint in him. He was suffering.... It took all day and all night... It was 35 to 40 below. You don't ever forget those things...."*

— *Grandpa Monk recalling a train accident near Langworthy.*

My grandpa John used to tell us stories from his days growing up on the farm two miles west of Langworthy. One of the stories was about a train wreck just south of town. If I heard that story once, I heard it fifty times. In 1999, I took a tape recorder with me when I stopped for a visit. I wanted to get the train story and others like it recorded as a keepsake. In 2007, I stumbled across that tape and listened to it again. You can hear the coffee pot percolating in the background the first several minutes.

In the interview, I asked grandpa about the train wreck, farming with horses, and making moonshine, etc....

Grandpa told me something I'd never heard before. He gave me the family recipe for making moonshine (which I've included later in the book).

The interview lasted about 40 minutes. It is priceless to me now that he is gone. After the interview was over, I decided to do an internet search on the local history of Langworthy, Monticello and Anamosa, Iowa. I came across the account of Marcus L. Hansen and John E. Briggs walking into Monticello in 1920. Their story was written by Hansen and Briggs in *The Palimpsest.* (1) Hansen and Briggs traced the route of something called "the Old Military Road" and mentioned a man by the name of Lyman Dillon. It seemed Dillon had plowed a furrow to mark the surveyed route of a new road. His plow (called a breaking plow), was attached to five yoke of oxen. That's ten oxen yoked together, a set up that was probably close to 60 feet in length.

I tried to imagine what it must have been like to break virgin sod in the sweltering heat of Iowa in August of 1839. At this point in American history, Iowa was on the edge of the American frontier. Dillon would have been surrounded by wolves and black bear, and witnessing Native Americans being forced off their land....Wow!

By the time I finished reading Hansen's and Briggs's account, an idea began to take shape. It had been eighty eight years since Hansen and Briggs' walk. I wondered to myself, what if I could walk that route?

And if I were to do it, I wanted to learn as much as I could about early Eastern Iowa history.

I spent 2007 immersed in the stories of life along the Old Military Road. My wife, Micaela, and my former art teacher, Joy Adams, joined me in this adventure. We purchased old maps, out of print county history books, and anything else which might give us clues into life in Eastern Iowa from 1839 to 1900.

In my search for old books, I had a chance encounter with Pam Foley at her antique store in Monticello. Pam shared that her dad, Gus Norlin, had also spent considerable time researching Lyman Dillon and the Old Military Road. She asked me if I would be interested in looking through his many newspaper clippings and personal correspondence on the topic. I have included some of that material in Chapter 7.

In order to make these stories flow together in a logical sequence, I'm going to tell them to you based on the route itself. I've decided to include what I know about Lyman Dillon in Chapter 4 since he was from Cascade.

There have already been many wonderful books written about the early life of Iowa City and Dubuque, some of which I read extensively in preparation for my walk. I do not plan to repeat the material that is in them since most of them are still in print and readily available. Rather, I have decided to focus on a couple of individuals and events in each town whose stories really grabbed my attention.

It's now 2016. Eight years since my walk. What follows are the highlights of my research as well as some of my thoughts while I walked.

I have to make some disclaimers and then proceed. I am not a formally trained historian. I am a carpenter who just happens to love local history and who just happens to have grown up along the route Lyman Dillon would have passed.

Secondly, I need to address my intentional decision to liberally quote from the original sources I acquired in preparation for my walk. I've decided rather than just summarize the material in my own words, I would include them verbatim. They are time capsules to the past.

Third, for personal reasons, I have included material about the Monk family in Chapter 3 that may be of little interest to anyone but my family.

This book is not intended to be a stuffy research book as much as a personal journal and a celebration of local history. If any of these stories stimulate new interest in our local history, then I will have accomplished my purpose.

*Douglas Monk,* February 2016

Federal roads in Iowa Territory are pictured in this map which appeared in the *Iowa Journal of History*, January, 1949.

*Federal roads in Iowa Territory map*

# Palimpsest article:

Here are portions of the Palimpsest article I came across on the internet that lit the fire for my journey:

*"Trailing diagonally across the state from Dubuque to Iowa City, is an old ridge road. It was laid out more than eighty years ago to connect the little mining town on the river with the new territorial capital. The United States government was then fostering the construction of military roads on the western frontier and in March, 1839. Congress appropriated twenty thousand dollars for such a road to begin at Dubuque and run "to such point on the northern boundary of the state of Missouri as may be best suited for its future extension by that state to the cities of Jefferson and St. Louis..."*

*"The road was ultimately extended beyond Iowa City, but to the people of the Territory of Iowa in 1839, the opportunity offered by the government meant simply access to the site of the new capital. The road from Dubuque as far as Iowa City was immediately surveyed. A United States army engineer named Tilghman, directing the work James, Lucius and Edward Langworthy, the first two of whom had crossed the Mississippi to the deserted diggings of Julien Dubuque in 1830, were given contracts for the construction of the road from Dubuque as far as the Cedar River. Edward Langworthy states that after the surveys were made, Tilghman engaged Lyman Dillon to plow a furrow along the route under his direction for the guidance of the contractors..."*

*"Meanwhile, at Iowa City, the town had been platted and the cap-itol building begun. A temporary tavern known as "Lean-back Hall", welcomed the travelers and tried to rival the hospitality which they had enjoyed at Tim Fanning's famous Log Tavern at the other end of the road. In the course of years, Tim Fanning's tavern and "Lean-back Hall" have disappeared, nevertheless, incentive was not lacking for two historically minded vacationists to retrace the old road on foot in September, 1920. The writers of the articles that follow, Marcus L. Hansen and John E. Briggs, set out one autumn morning from Iowa City equipped with stout shoes and hearts, a tiny tent, an ancient map, and all the information they could gather about the old highway. Four days they walked on the way to Dubuque, their feet treading the modern thoroughfare while their minds were busy with the traces of deserted villages and the ancient secrets of*

living towns, with the signs of departed traffic and the many reminders of the vanished spirits of the Old Military Road...."

"The Old Military Road! How foreign the expression to the peaceful, early autumn calm that lay over the valleys dropping away to the right and left of the ridge along which the road wound. My comrade and I had shouldered our packs at Iowa City and, setting our faces toward the Northeast, had begun with ambitious strides to walk the old thoroughfare from Iowa City to Dubuque—our only motive being that furnished by the old books which told us that so the pioneers of Iowa had done..."

"The Mississippi River towns were full of men eager to venture forth into the wilderness, and the Indian trails on the prairies were followed by the ever-moving pioneers. That these irrepressible spirits would soon come into forcible contact with the Indians who only reluctantly had left their homes in the ceded "Forty Mile Strip" seemed inevitable, and in order that the iron hand of the government might be felt in the remotest valleys, roads were necessary whereby troops might be readily sent from the permanent posts to the scene of any disturbance. That one of these should lead from Dubuque, the commercial and military center of the upper Mississippi, to Iowa City, the new capital, was logical and, by act of Congress in 1839, an appropriation was made to pay for the surveying, grading, and bridging of such a thoroughfare. Yet even from the first, the number of soldiers who passed over it was surpassed by the incoming swarm of settlers, and the military men did little more than leave their name upon their work..."

"And as such it is known to this day by all who dwell by its winding course. The college student who was painting the Ivanhoe Bridge laid down his brush—he was working for the county—and explained to us who pretended ignorance that the real designation of the trail we followed was the Military Road. The gray-headed sage at Monticello who gossiped with us as we stopped to rest our weary feet at the Depot Park declaimed on the sacrilege of rerouting a few miles of The Military Road as some moderns favored; and at the Trappist Abbey, kindhearted, Brother Timothy, he of the twinkling eyes, led us down to the pasture gate and with his walking stick pointed out a cross-cut by which we might regain The Military Road. All knew of the glory that once was the portion of the old highway..."

"Misery loves company and to console ourselves as the darkness gathered from the already gloomy valleys, we conjured up, one by one, *the shades of departed wanderers to accompany us — a procession of phantoms of the Old Military Road. They were travelers whose journey- ings have already been forgotten; Leather stockings who had no Cooper; black-robed priests without their Parkman; frontier Ichabods whose singing school escapades no Irving has recorded; horse-thieves who were hanged before the first dime novel was penned; all that motley band of men and women whose yellowed letters are still unread about the foundation stones of whose cabins the roots of lofty trees are now entwined, and many indeed who never wrote a letter, who never built a cabin but who, living, created that great romance that hovers about the wooded watercourses of Eastern Iowa, felt by everyone yet related by almost none. Among the throng are Edmund Booth and his two companions, who tell of how they passed this way long before the rivers were bridged, and when few fea- tures marked the passage across the seas of waving prairie grass.*

*Leaving Dubuque to make a residence in the west, they bid adieu to the sordid associations of "Dirty Hollow" and to the rippling waters of Catfish Creek with its busy mill, follow the dim trail that leads to the falls of the Maquoketa where already a few cabins cluster about the charming Cascade. Here and there are wagon ruts to guide their horses' feet along the winding ridge that, like a huge serpent, crawls on its way to the ford over the south fork of the Maquoketa. And now, the lights streaming out between the logs of the cabin of Daniel Varvel—first resident of Monticel- lo, betoken a supper of ham and eggs, corn dodgers and coffee, and a bed in the fragrant hay piled high in the rude barn.*

*Early the next morning, they are off again for there are streams to be crossed (Kitty's Creek and Fawn Creek), before the site of Anamosa is reached on the banks of the Wapsipinicon River. Booth goes no further but his two companions, bound for Iowa City, continue their way over the rolling prairie that stretches on to the waters of the Cedar..."*

*"Yonder in our procession of phantoms is one driving five yoke of oxen attached to a plow. Lyman Dillon is his name, and if the story of Dillon and his furrow had not been somewhat discredited by the historical critics, his would have been the most honored position in the group. For the old tradition relates that it was he who first rescued travelers from the dangers of waywardness. Employed by citizens of Iowa City, with his oxen and plow, he threw a furrow almost a hundred miles long extending from the capital to Dubuque, and the wagons and riders that followed this guide, beat a road by its side which was the predecessor of the Military Road. However, though the records have made mythical parts of this tradition,*

*he claims a role among these characters..."*

"On an autumn day three years before the Old Military Road was established, Daniel Varvel, a valiant native of Kentucky, came to the mouth of Kitty Creek on the south fork of the Maquoketa River. The view that greeted his eyes was surpassingly beautiful. Then and there he decided to build his new home. Jack Frost had already painted the well wooded hill sides with gorgeous splashes of crimson and yellow and brown. Over the hills the fertile prairie extended beyond the horizon. No home seeker had appeared there before. No axe had disturbed the wild solitude and no plowshare had ripped through the sod.

For years, the Varvel log cabin was a landmark in Jones County. The wayfaring traveler stopped there for the night. It served as headquarters for the men who laid out the old road, the mail that came once a week, was thrown off there. One by one, other cabins were built in the neighborhood. A two-story hotel about twenty feet square was erected. The settlement grew and came to be called Monticello. The traveler who now visits the flourishing city can scarcely imagine such humble beginnings. Gone long ago are the trails of the Indian and the smoke of his wigwam. Gone too are the primitive methods of travel and with them, perhaps, the spirit of fine hospitality.

John E. Briggs and Marcus L. Hansen

*A little cascade in the north branch of the Maquoketa River was a natural allurement for millers. As early as 1844, two pairs of burrs made of limestone were busily grinding "very superior flour." Within a few years, Cascade was a prosperous village. While the stage coach stopped for an hour at Steel's Tavern, the enterprising young real estate dealers boomed corner lots to the agents of eastern investors. What a glorious future for a town, they said, where the power from a waterfall nine feet in height was available! To this day, at least one lot is owned by the heirs of those early speculators. But alas, more than water is needed to make a great city." (1)*

The author, coming up Whiskey Hill in Dubuque, following
in the footsteps of Briggs and Hansen, who were following
the trail of Lyman Dillon.

# 1

# Iowa City To Solon

### September 8, 2008

Illiam McCormick describes the Iowa City area seen by the first pioneers:

*"How well do I remember Iowa City in its pristine beauty, with all its surroundings, its rolling prairies, its lovely groves of timber, and its crooked, meandering river, winding its way through the undulating hills, and luxuriantly, grass-covered prairies of Iowa, emptying its waters into the great Mississippi. Johnson County was then a wilderness, the very confines of civilization, the home of the red men, and of the howling prairie wolf. In 1839, I first arrived there, but few settlers at that time, a log cabin, dotted here and there the margin of the timber land, among which McCrory's and Trowbridge's 8x10 was most conspicuous. And I can remember well of sitting in one corner of it on a log, and eating roast potatoes from the ashes, broiled bacon from spit. I think we had a little "Cincinnati, double-rectified from a jug."(a)*

Today is September 8th, 2008. There is a slight drizzle as I get out of our white Toyota Camry in downtown Iowa City.

"All the better, I think to myself... it just adds to this adventure."
On the northeast corner of Clinton and Washington, the Daughters of the American Revolution have attached a bronze marker to the concrete wall. It reads: *Iowa City stage stop on the Old Military Road from Dubuque to the northern boundary of the Missouri authorized by Congress, 1839.* Today is the day I've chosen to begin my walk back in time, retracing Lyman Dillon and the furrow that he plowed. I've been preparing for this adventure for one and one-half years, preparation in the form of research - not physical, I am not a walker. I am a general contractor. I frame houses, pour concrete, and shingle roofs. By the end of most work days, I'm physically exhausted, so taking a walk to "stay in shape" is the last thing on my mind. The only physical training I've done is purchase a good pair

of running shoes.

As I take off, I think to myself; "Can I really pull this off? Can I walk 80 some miles in six days without any special training? What if I get blisters? What if I pull a muscle? I don't want to do something stupid that will haunt me the rest of my life."

At the same time, there is also a profound sense of peace, so I push the "what ifs" out of my mind and savor the moment.

A small city park diagonally across the street with the name Chauncey Swan catches my eye. I know that name. Chauncey Swan was one of the big shakers and movers in the very earliest days of Iowa City. He was just one of many people I felt like I'd gotten to know this past year.

As I turn the corner and continue to walk north on Dodge Street, I think to myself; "Slow down, I'll be on the edge of town before I know it and into the open country."

---

## Chauncey Swan

1799–1852
(He died at sea, coming home from the California Gold Rush)

*"Chauncey Swan was a man who would have known Old Military Road well, even in its very first creation. Swan had made the trip from Dubuque as one of the early legislators to Burlington, probably by river boat. But later in the session, he had traveled from Burlington to mark out the original town and future site of the Iowa seat of government. One cannot predict with any certainty where the future lies, but every step of Chauncey Swan's life from the moment he stood looking at his watch waiting for a wayward commissioner to arrive to legally make this place the official*

*location for the seat of government was going to be monumental for him. Chauncey tired of the political to and fro, but he had resigned himself to create a great place for the Iowa Legislature to meet. Although no longer in politics, he took on the task of building and contracting for the capital building. Swan would be treated with little respect and often would have his budgets reduced after having contracted for services. He managed to pull through it all, build a very distinctive capital building and on top of that, operate a first class pioneer hotel, and master the postal system. Swan laid out the town and made places for a number of church denominations, green spaces and markets. When he left the place for the Gold Rush, it was a much finer place than when he had first arrived. It sported a saw mill that he had created along with his hotel, state capital and a fine city plan. His investment was dear, he lost his first wife and only daughter, both buried in the Iowa City cemetery. He, on the other hand, would be buried at sea, no marker for his grave, but a small park in the town he had worked so diligently for, his only physical manifestation." (b)*

Chauncey Swan came from New York state to Iowa with his wife, Dolly, and their four children hoping to make money working the lead mines of Dubuque.

In September, 1838, Swan was elected to the House of the first territorial legislature. In the summer of 1839, Swan moved with his family to Iowa City. That summer, Swan oversaw the surveys, chose the spot for Capitol Square, and arranged for maps to be made and coordinated land sales which began in August, 1839.

Swan contended with many setbacks in the building of the capitol. The biggest setback was when the contractor, John F. Rague, quit the project entirely. Swan then added to his duties the responsibilities of building contractor, including hiring and paying workers, drawing up contracts, purchasing materials, and supervising day-to-day construction. (As a contractor myself, I can't imagine the herculean task that would have involved). Perhaps most frustrating for Swan, was the legislature's lack of trust in him.

In December, 1839, the legislature asked for copies of contracts and financial records. The following year, they sent investigators to evaluate the capitol's progress and review Swan's bookkeeping. No accusations of mismanagement were leveled against him, but in January 1841, the legislature divided the responsibilities of Acting Commissioner and created the positions of Territorial Agent, responsible for project finances and Superintendent of Public Buildings, responsible for supervising the capitol's construction. Governor Lucas appointed Swan Superintendent of Public Buildings, a position he held until February 1842.

In 1843, he was an organizer and president of the Iowa City Manufacturing Company, which built a dam and gristmill along the Iowa River near present-day Coralville. Unfortunately, within two years the company was bankrupt, and the dam and mill were sold.

In 1849, he left for California in search of gold. He mined until early 1852. Letters to his wife, Mary (he had remarried), suggest that he had some success. On his return home from the California Gold Rush, he died at sea; age 53. (3)

---

## Phillip Clark

Phillip Clark. It is funny how many times his name surfaced in early *Iowa City History.*

Phillip Clark and Eli Myers were two of the first young men to stake claims in the Iowa City area in the fall of 1836. Of all the early stories I came across in the Iowa City area (and there are several), the account of Phillip Clark's sister going into labor gripped me the most:

(5) Mrs. Smith, a young woman, probably in her late teens or early 20s, had followed her brother, Phillip Clark, west the summer of 1838 with her husband Patrick. They were living in a crude claim cabin, a shelter not more than twelve to fourteen feet square. She went into labor in early August. The closest doctor was forty miles away in Muscatine. She had complications, and suffered for two days in the sweltering heat, unable to deliver the baby.

Finally a neighbor, S.C. Trowbridge, started for Muscatine to fetch the doctor.

Before he left for Muscatine, Trowbridge met some local Native Americans from Wapashasheik's village. He told them about the young white woman in labor. These "savages" head back to their village and tell their midwives. The midwives immediately gather wild herbs and roots from which they make a concoction for her to drink. A few minutes later, the baby is safely delivered. That story really touched me. It puts a whole different perspective on the relationship between the early settlers and Iowa's native populations.

## The Ride

May 1st, 1839. The date set aside to stake out the location for the new territorial capital building (we know it as, "Old Capital" today).

As more and more people poured into the Iowa Territory, the powers that be decide it would be good to locate the center of government further west and so the site of Iowa City is selected. But according to the rule, there needed to be at least two territorial commissioners present at this meeting. The problem is, there was only one...Chauncey Swan.

(7) "...As noonday approached, and no other commissioner appeared, the crowd began to suspect fraud. Burlington and the counties in the Southeastern part of the territory were bitterly opposed to locating the seat of government in Johnson County. It was thought that an attempt had been made to prevent a majority of commissioners from meeting. There was now excitement and alarm lest the entire county should be cheated out of the prized location...."

Chauncey Swan mounted a dry-goods box and made a short speech to the agitated crowd....

Iowa City would forfeit the right to be the new territorial capital unless a second commissioner could be found – before twelve midnight.

The closest commissioner was John Ronalds, who lived thirty five miles south in Lousia County. Someone needed to make a seventy mile round trip on horseback and fetch Ronalds, and be back before midnight. Keep in mind this was 1839. There were no roads. The last several hours of the return trip would be complete darkness.

Phillip Clark steps forward. He volunteers to make the trip.

In the end, Clark and Ronalds did make it back, although there is some question whether they really made it back by twelve midnight or the hands on Swan's watch were "adjusted" just a little.

## A California Widow and The Lynching Bee

In 1844, Phillip Clark married a Miss Clarissa Lee. Six years later in 1850, Clark left with his old buddy, Eli Myers for the gold fields of California. The gold bug had bitten again.

For seven years, his wife heard nothing from him. Nothing! She did not know whether he was alive or dead. She became what was known in those days as a "California Widow."

Clarissa finally filed papers to divorce Clark on the ground of desertion. She sold the 742 acres of her former husband's estate. In 1857, Clark rode back into town...

(8) "In 1857, Philip Clark returned and immediately commenced proceedings for the recovery of his farm. ...he built a cabin and stable on the land and made his home there. "Possession is nine points of the law," say the lawyers and he thus took possession. A notorious bad character named Boyd Wilkinson, had a "possession" cabin on another part of the farm, holding it in the interest of the ex-Mrs. Clark. The parties to whom she had sold the land, and two lawyers, W. Penn Clarke and F.H. Lee. Wilkinson was under indictment for grand larceny....but was out on bail till the June session of court. W. Penn Clarke, as attorney for the divorced woman and those to whom she had sold the land, wanted to oust Philip Clark from his actual "possession" of the land which gave him a good deal of advantage in the lawsuits he had instituted for the recovery of his title. From all the circumstances it would seem that Wilkinson was employed to so pester, annoy and injure old Philip as to scare or drive him off from that land.

One night, Wilkinson and two others, attacked Mr. Clark on his road home, beating and bruising him severely.

Clark had Wilkinson arrested for this outrage, fined, and put under bonds to keep the peace, but the lawyer, W. Penn Clarke, obtained his release. And shortly after, on the night of May 10, 1858, Philip Clark's barn was burned down, along with a pair of horses.

It was firmly believed by Philip and his friends that Wilkinson had done it.

At this point a mob forms… "they go to Wilkinson's house in that state of fury and desperation which men sometimes reach when sharp criminal lawyers succeed in baffling the good intent of protective laws until there is left no resource of redress but the bad and dangerous lynch power.

From circumstances under which he was living on Philip Clark's land, they had abundance of "mob-reason" to believe him guilty.

They first tried to frighten Wilkinson into a confession, but failed. Then they tied his hands behind his back, boosting him into a hack and started off, most likely with the intention of not killing him outright, but of "playing hang" with him until he confessed; though in fact they went directly to the river bank, and may have intended to dunk instead of choke.

At any rate, they were out on a lynching bee; they were terribly in earnest and they meant to use him rough. There was no kid-glove delicacy in that crowd; they told him they were going to hang him, and he believed it.

But instead, he drowns and those who had him in charge at the time, always claimed that he jumped into the river. He was noted as a good swimmer, but his hands were tied and he sunk at once. It might easily be, however, that in the intense excitement of the moment he forgot this and though if he jumped into the river he could swim across and get away from them." This occurred about two miles below the city on May 11th, 1858.

Back to the present; It's now 2008, day one of my adventure. My goal is to make it to Solon and spend the night with Ron and Mary Hulubar. I look like the hunchback of Notre Dame with a big yellow rain coat as I head north on Highway 1. I have a small backpack with a bladder of Gatorade under my rain coat.

I'd learned my lesson in 2007. In 2007, I did a practice walk from Iowa City to Solon just to see if I had the stamina. The day of my practice walk, I had not taken anything with me to drink (in spite of my wife's suggestion), so by the time I arrived in Solon, I was thirsty. I had also brought along a plastic garbage bag to pick up empty cans that day, thinking it would help me pass the time, but by the time I arrived in Solon, I had a large bag of cans that were really slowing me down.

A couple good things came out of that 2007 practice walk. First, I learned I needed something to drink, and secondly, don't pick up cans. As noble of an idea as it sounded, it took too much energy.

As I get to the north edge of Iowa City, Joy Adams caught up with me. She had offered to take pictures periodically throughout my walk. Halfway to Solon, I lost her. I had turned down a couple of miles of winding gravel road called Dillon's Furrow. This road was a peaceful break from the fast moving two lane traffic of Highway 1. As I get to the end of "Dillon's Furrow Road," I call Joy to see where she is. We realize she'd parked on the stretch of Highway 1 that ran parallel to the gravel road I'd just walked. I tell her to head north and look for me on the right.

My friend, Dave Berryann, catches up with me as I waited for Joy. Dave had carved a walking stick with a hoof on the bottom for my trip and brought it to me. We took a few pictures when Joy arrived, then I'm off.

As Solon comes into view, a car pulls over in front of me; someone jumped out and asks, "Are you that guy walking Old Military Road?"

Her name is Pat. She'd read about my trip and is out placing political signs for the upcoming presidential election between Barack Obama and John McCain.

I stop at the Dairy Mart on the edge of Solon to grab a bite to eat with Joy before heading into the town square of Solon. I am scheduled to meet Sandy Hanson, Milli Gilbaugh and Doug Lindner from The Solon Economist around 3:30 p.m. - 4:00 p.m. for a photo shoot.

As we stand in the town square, Sandy and Milli describe how the original route would have come into town further south and west, went past the train depot then headed past the current Methodist Church, and exited Solon over a bridge that is now closed.

We jump into a couple of vehicles and head to the church where there is a historical marker placed by an Eagle Scout.

It's 4:30 p.m. and I walk to the home of Ron and Mary Holubar where I will spend the night. Mary is the sister of Larry Pisarik, a friend of mine. Larry and his wife Kathy, were instrumental in helping me find lodging for several nights of my walk.

In an earlier conversation, Larry had mentioned to me how Solon, Iowa and Langworthy, Iowa, are "related" in a historical sort of way. Solon is named after Solon Langworthy - one of the four Langworthy brothers from Dubuque and Langworthy obviously is the last name of that prominent family.

Ironically, Kathy Pisarik (Larry's wife), is a direct descendant of the Langworthy family. I plan to tell you a little bit more about the Langworthy family as we get near Dubuque.

As I settle in this first evening of my walk, I am very thankful for the Holubar's hospitality. Until a few weeks before, it looked like I was going to spend my first night in a tent at the historical stone school house north of Solon. Considering the fact that it had drizzled off and on and more rain is expected overnight, I am thankful to be sleeping inside this family's home.

Showing hospitality to complete strangers was a common practice in 1839, and I am happy and relieved it is still being practiced in 2008.

Raphael Pisarik (Larry's dad), is a local historian. He pays me a visit this first night of my walk. I finish my first evening sitting around the Holubar kitchen table listening to stories of local history from a man who knows what he is talking about.

*Raphael Pisarik and I sharing stories around the kitchen table. September 8, 2008*

# 2

# Solon To Mount Vernon

## September 9, 2008

It is still dark as I said good bye to Ron Holubar. I have been invited to speak in Mount Vernon this morning. Mr. Ed Timm, a ninth grade history teacher, had read about my journey retracing the Old Military Road in *The (Cedar Rapids) Gazette* and asked if I could stop by his class on my way through town. The students were studying the Military Road as part of a local history unit study. I want to get to Mount Vernon before 11 a.m. if it is to work out. There is a heavy fog in the air as I leave town. I take pictures of a grain setup peeking through the fog in the distance and the stone school house I had initially thought I would be sleeping at.

*Grain setup in the distance*

*Stone School house just north of Solon.*

As I continue north on Highway 1, I come to the Cedar River. My mind goes to the stories Raphael had told me the night before— the area was once thick with horse thieves, counterfeiters and wolves. Here is a story that made the hair on the back of my neck stand up...

# The Big White Wolf

"It was known far and wide as "the big white wolf," and made its appearance first about 1850, and was seen from time to time for several years in the eastern and southern parts of the township and in various other localities. It was seen by many persons, and many more desired to see the wonderful creature.

From the description given by those who saw it, it was known to be an animal of the "wolf" kind, though unlike anything seen by any person in this vicinity. Such was its strength that it would and did carry off full grown sheep with perfect ease, and of all the numerous dogs which attacked it none could make any impression upon it, but were handled as a mastiff handles a terrier.

Many attempts were made to kill or capture the beast, but he was exceedingly wary so that few persons ever got within gun-shot of him. He was caught in a trap by Jonathon Talbott, and carried the trap many miles, but finally escaped, losing a toe, as was discovered by his tracks when he next appeared in this locality, which was not for several months. Poison was tried freely upon him, but the dose which would "lay out" a "coyote," would have no effect upon him. At last, however, he was brought to bay and disposed of by John E. Douglass, now a resident of Oxford, and J.J. Shepardson, now living in Clear Creek Township. He was caught in two traps, they being fastened together by a log-chain to which was attached a heavy "blacksmith's sledge." The traps were set for him near the Douglass place, and as soon as it was ascertained that they "had him," they started in pursuit with four good dogs, which finally succeeded in stopping him till the men came up, when they had reached a point on Clear Creek nearly south of the present site of Oxford, a distance of more than three miles. Here they had him in the water and the fight raged furiously - the men being unable to "get in a shot" without danger of killing a dog. As fast as the animal would try to climb the bank the dogs would pull him back, when the fight would be renewed in the water, until the dogs were beaten off and the wolf would again attempt to escape. Finally, Shepardson went down into the water to see what aid he could give the dogs, and just at the time the wolf became disengaged from the trap and started up the bank and escape seemed certain. But Joe was equal to the occasion, seizing the animal by the tail and reaching forward, he gave him several vigorous stabs with his pocket knife, which ended his career. His size exceeded the apparently exaggerated reports given by those who had seen him alive, being four feet and three inches high, though rather short in proportion. His weight was proportionate to his size, but not definitely known. The hair, which was white, tipped with a steel gray, was from four to five inches in length and as thick as the wool on a sheep. His legs were of the size of a muscular man's arm and his paws like those of a lion. That the skin was not saved and properly mounted is much to be regretted."

## Horse Thieves

One of the horse thieves in the area was a Mr. John Brodie. Brodie moved to Linn County about 1840 from Ohio; he came because it was remote. If you were a homesteader, you never knew when one of your horses might turn up missing. The big woods were the perfect hideout for men like Brodie and his boys, John Jr., Stephen, William, Hugh, and Jesse.

Some of the other worthless scoundrels in the area included Sam Leterel, Christian Grove, James Case (also known as Jim Stulenburg), a Mr. McConlogue, Mr. Squires, and a Mr. McBroom.

11 p.m., April 14, 1840, five men broke into the home of John Goudy. It had been rumored that Goudy had $9,000.00 stashed somewhere in his cabin. Keep in mind, a day's wage was less than a dollar; that pencils out to $1,500.00 a year-gross. $9,000.00 would be the equivalent to $144,000.00 in today's money. The thieves demanded to know where the $9,000.00 was. Goudy said he didn't have that kind of money. The thieves went through every inch of the cabin. They found $120.00 from Goudy's daughter Hannah. After threatening the family, the thieves headed down the road to the home of William F. Gilbert.

It just so happened that the Gilbert family had company staying with them; the Dubuque and Iowa City mail carrier and two other men. Gilbert and the mail carrier were asleep on the floor in front of the door. Mrs. Gilbert and her children were in one of the beds and the other two men were in the other. The thieves broke in so quickly they took all of them by surprise. Mr. Gilbert and the mail carrier tried to defend the cabin but were quickly beaten down with a club. They found a total of $240.00. Mr. Gilbert's son recognized a neighbor (a Mr. Goodrich) as one of the gang.

I came across another version of that crime spree from the Centennial

*"By 1842, horse thieves were so common that settlers had to keep their barns locked at night. Notably, the Brodies were the tough gang who stole from cabins and broke up social dances. They came from the deep woods over by Linn Grove. They broke into the Goudy cabin over north, at night, brandishing a gun and demanding the $9,000.00 Mr. Goudy had brought from the east. They found only $120.00 in a pocket book and went on to rob the neighbors. Later, the vigilantes got two of the gang and flogged them on their bare backs until they fainted. There was not much government but plenty of rude justice in these prairies and woods."*

*Making a presentation to Mr. Timm's class*

Coming back to the present, I do make it to Mr. Timm's history class, and get the chance to speak to three groups of students.

While I'm there, I ask the students if they can tell me any local history stories. They tell me several stories - one about three of the Brodie brothers who were caught with stolen horses in their possession and, within 30 minutes, all three were swinging from a tree - hanged! Now that story, while I didn't come across it in anything I'd read, does correspond with what I had heard about the Brodie family.

As you come into Mount Vernon today, try to imagine what it would have looked like in 1840:

*"Prairie grass grew rank and high over the wind-swept hilltop of what is now Mount Vernon. Tall elms, oaks, linden trees, perhaps a hundred years old grew on the west slope of the hill; and a less coverage of wild plum and crabapple trees sent forth delicious aroma in the spring. At the foot of the east end of the hill, was a copious spring of water where travelers would stop to quench their thirst. A rough trail, widened by "stone boats" which oxen pulled, ran steeply up the present schoolhouse hill and over to the west. Smoke from Daniel Hahn's cabin to the south floated lazily over the hilltop.*

*The Military Road from Iowa City to Dubuque had been surveyed and a furrow ploughed by Lyman Dillon with five yoke of oxen marked the road over the winding hilltop." (11)*

September 9 is a big day for me. After speaking to the high school classes, Micaela and I make a stop by a historical marker placed by the *Daughters of the American Revolution.* In Mount Vernon, we have a second photo shoot. After pictures, we jump in a car with Dorothy Rilett (my host for the night), and Joy Adams. We drive to Cedar Rapids where I have the opportunity to speak to a group at Cottage Grove Place about this history project. When Dorothy Rilett first got wind of my walk, she said to me, "Well, when you get to Mount Vernon, you have a place to stay." I so appreciated her gracious spirit and gift of hospitality.

*Dorothy Rilett serving us breakfast day 3 of my walk.*

# 3

# Mount Vernon to Anamosa

September 10, 2008

*Jerry Hiner and I at Gordon Lumber Company 2008*

I wake up refreshed Wednesday morning. On the north edge of town before leaving Mount Vernon, I stop by Gordon Lumberyard to say "hi" to Jerry Hiner. I am due in Martelle mid-morning.

I've been invited to speak at the senior center as well as take pictures by the Dillon's Furrow marker on the edge of town.

Before arriving in Martelle, I spot John Tasker, a friend who works for the state mowing ditches. He offers me a Hostess Twinkie and a Pepsi.

As Martelle comes into view, I remember a comment by Joy Adams. She'd said she always wanted to take a picture of the grain silos as you come into town from the south. They seem to come right out of the road... so as they come into view, I do just that; I get into the middle of Highway 1 and take some quick pictures.

I arrive in Martelle around 10 am. KWWL – channel 7 TV station from Waterloo, calls me on my cell phone and asks if they could interview me and take some footage of me walking. I agree to hang around Martelle until they arrive. At the senior center I give a brief presentation, get a foot

*Martelle grain silos coming into view.*

*Betty Johnson giving me a foot massage in Martelle*

*Historical marker in Martelle Iowa with local group of history lovers.*

massage by Betty Johnson, and am presented with a blue T-shirt commemorating Martelle, Iowa. I love every minute of this adventure.

After the reception and TV interview, I'm anxious to be off. I still have a good three hours of walking ahead of me.

In my mind's eye, I try to imagine the timber line ahead of me. North of Martelle, the land would have been prairie grass and slough. As I get closer to Fairview, I try to imagine the 30 log cabins nestled against the timber line that stretched from Highland Point (to the east, to Viola to the west).

As I come to the intersection of Highway 1 and 151, I want to continue north under the overpass into the town of Fairview. Over the years, the original route of the Military Road has been gradually straightened. In 1839, the route of the road followed the contour of the ground and stuck to the natural ridges of the land.

Coming into Fairview, I remember this description of what it would have looked like in the mid 1800s. I came across the following article which originally appeared in the *Anamosa Eureka* dated October 28, 1909:

*"In a recent interview with Mr. Hiram Joslin, who landed in Jones County, August 27, 1837, he narrated some of the experiences of himself and other members of the family. In those days deer, elk, wild turkeys, etc, were very plentiful everywhere, particularly in the Big Woods, as the Wapsie timber belt was called. Mr. John G. Joslin, the father of Hiram, Clark, Harrison, Daniel, Thurston and their sisters, we remember well as*

*a great hunter, and many a deer, elk and wild turkey fell before his un-
erring rifle. All the boys, and in fact, most of the old settlers, were more
or less given to exploits of this character. Mr. Hiram Joslin claims the
honor of having shot the biggest deer ever killed in the county. Mr. Miles
Russell, another old hunter remembered by a few, was with Mr. Joslin
at the time. They were one and a half miles Northwest of Fairview when
Hiram finally brought down the big buck. The buck's mate was with him
and was followed a short distance and shot, the ball cutting the big artery.
Hiram then went home, southeast of Fairview, hitched a yoke of oxen to
a sled, and, with this father accompanying him, drove two or three miles,
loaded up the game and hauled it in. The buck weighed over four hundred
pounds, and in all probability, as Mr. Joslin says, was the largest ever captured in this locality. Hiram gave the skins to his father, who had learned
from the Indians the art of dressing and tanning them for clothing, which
we remember to have seen worn frequently. Mr. Joslin said the buckskin
suit was "a little sticky when wet but lasted long - too long, sometimes to
suit him."*

*Mr. Joslin recalled a fishing trip in which he, his brothers John and
Harrison, their father, and George and Eli Brown, joined. While on their
way to the Wapsi, they ran on a couple of elk. The Brown's had a rifle
and shot the biggest of the pair, but the other waded across the river and
escaped. After dark, two torches were set aflame and borne quietly along
the shore. John Joslin speared a sturgeon weighing sixty pounds. This
was their biggest prize, but before they concluded their night's sport, they
had also captured six or eight muskellunge and when they were hung on
poles suspended on their shoulders, some of their tails touched the ground.
This is not an incredible story by any means. For we remember to have
seen muskellunge weighing from twenty-two to twenty-eight pounds and
have known of their being occasionally taken that weighed thirty to forty
pounds, a fact that Mr. Joslin, we doubt not, can corroborate from his
personal knowledge.*

*Wild geese, ducks and pigeons in their season by the millions and prai-
rie chickens and quail innumerable- a mere mention is sufficient, for they
were a drug in the market. But those days are gone, never to return..."(12)*

As I pass the Baptist Church on my left in Fairview, a motorcyclist
pulls over in front of me and offers to give me a ride. I tell him thanks for
the offer but I'm good. There used to be more to Fairview than there is
today. I take a picture of a building foundation on my right. From my reading and talking with Joy Adams, that building may have been a stagecoach

*Ford House, Anamosa, Iowa 2008*

stop. It's 3:30 p.m. as I come into Anamosa, down the long hill past the state park. It is here I experience the only real physical discomfort of my whole walk. The back of my legs tighten up coming down the long grade.

Joy Adams meets me on the edge of Anamosa; we take some photos by some blue stem prairie grass at the entrance to the state park, and then take a quick walk over to another historical marker - The Ford House, where the Indian princess, Anamosa, and her parents once visited. Becky, from the Anamosa paper, had suggested to Joy that originally, main street (and the Military Road), would very likely have passed this house and headed behind the Anamosa Cemetery, avoiding the steep hill I had walked down into town. Joy and I look to the south and can very easily imagine Becky is probably right.

I stop at the office of the *Anamosa Eureka* where Becky has some questions for me to answer while the video camera is running. After I finish my walk, I sent Becky a CD with the photo highlights of the trip. She created a DVD with my interview, the photos, and some music.

As I read about the early history of Anamosa, one man in particular stuck out. His name was Edmund Booth.

Cecilia Hatcher was the first person from Anamosa to tell me about Edmund Booth. I had stopped at her antique store in search of old history books. She sold me the two volume *Jones County History* published in 1910. (13)

*Becky Dirks Haugsted and Joy Adams at the Anamosa Eureka*

*Edmund Booth*

*Mary Ann Walworth Booth*

Edmund Booth was deaf, but accomplished more in his lifetime than most of us do who can hear.

As the following accounts will explain, he was a teacher in a deaf school in Hartford, Connecticut. While teaching there, he met a young woman by the name of Mary Ann Walworth, who was one of his students.

As I was talking with Becky at the Anamosa Local Access channel about Booth, she suggested (and I think she's right), that Edmund was smitten by the young Mary and had followed her halfway across the United States. When Edmund caught up with her, she was 40 miles west of the Mississippi on the edge of the western frontier helping her sister cook and clean for 18 men (including her brother), building a new mill on Buffalo Creek near the present town of Anamosa.

I received this account of the life of Edmund Booth from Steve Hanken: (14) Edmund Booth, 1810-1905. The Life Story Of a Deaf Pioneer.

*He was born in Chicopee, Massachusetts, August 24, 1810. His father was a farmer. The family was able to trace their ancestry back to 1275 in England.*

*In 1815, his father died suddenly from a disease considered contagious. Three days later, Edmund was attacked by the same disease....took the form of total loss of sight in one eye, and partial deafness. Three years later, when he was eight years old, he lost his hearing completely, but by that time he had fortunately learned a little reading, writing and speech. His speech organs were normal, and his conversational powers in adult life were considered remarkable. His autobiographical notes, written after he had reached 75 when his diary was thought to be lost and his letters of Gold Rush days were not known to have been preserved; Booth describes how he learned to read:*

*"I have a dim recollection of my mother taking a straw from the broom, setting me on her lap and pointing to each letter of the alphabet and naming it. This was soon after my father's death or when I was four or five years old....Mother afterwards said she sent me to school but the teachers said they could not teach me, so she took me on her lap and taught me the one-syllable words, ba, be, bi, bo etc. I could hear a little in the left ear at the time and until eight years, when my hearing left me in the night."*

*All of his early schooling was at home. In 1828, when Edmund was 16, he entered the Hartford (Connecticut) school which was called an "asylum" and seems to have been an institution operated by a private corpora-*

tion for the education of the deaf and dumb. It was not an insane asylum, nor were there any mental defectives there. Before Booth completed his education at the "asylum," he was asked to begin teaching classes, and this work was continued until he resigned in May, 1839. One of his pupils was Mary Ann Walworth, 14 years old, (in 1831) who, years later, would become his wife. She was a deaf-mute who had become deaf at the age of 4, following an illness.

Booth's autobiographical notes are as follows:

"In June 1839 I left the Hartford school by the regular stage coach for Albany, New York. Traveled all night and nearly all the next day. At Albany, stopped at the Eagle tavern. An hour or two later, took railroad cars for Syracuse. Arriving at Syracuse I learned I could go on by stage or by canal to Oswego on Lake Ontario. I chose the latter with a view to get sight of the renowned lake....Late in the afternoon the regular steamer arrived from Kingston, Canada, and I went aboard for Lewiston, situated at the mouth of the Niagara River. In the morning we reached Lewiston, entered the river.....On the American side we left the boat and climbed the steep bank. A railroad train of two or three coaches was waiting. The town was almost nothing. The train stopped at Niagara Falls and I gave the whole place a full inspection.....in the afternoon another train started for Buffalo. At that time the only railroads west of New York City or Albany were from Albany to Syracuse and from Lockport to Buffalo. Frink's mud wagons, were the mail stages of this western section were called were the only sure means of conveyance...Five days were consumed in a pleasant lake voyage to Chicago with brief stops at Detroit and Milwaukee. Chicago seemed to be but a few feet above the water. It was a straggling town, buildings of frame here and there, to the view hardly twenty buildings in all....entering one of the stores, saw an Indian, painted and standing motionless like a statue, stern looking and leaning against a pile of goods. Town lots were cheap as low as $75.00 each. In the afternoon took stage, one of Frink and Walker's mud wagons, for Galena on the river by that name. Reached Galena at noon, larger than Chicago, better built, regular streets and apparently far more population. Went in The Gazette newspaper office, procured a couple of papers and mailed to Sister Hannah in Springfield Massachusetts. At the post office, as I delivered the papers, the two young men in attendance looked at me suspiciously as I thought. Supposed it was perhaps some revelation of western manners. Returned to the hotel for dinner. Found the piazza filled with a crowd, all gazing at me as though they thought me an ogre. Found dinner nearly over. Took a seat at the table. The landlord placed before me what was wanted, and I began to eat. Soon a big, burly man entered, stood by my side and spoke orally. I made the usual sign of want of hearing and went on with my dinner. By this time a crowd was standing around in front. A minute or two passed thus and then the burly looking fellow beside me (suppose he had been speaking and getting no answer) tossed a handbill by my plate. It described a murderer in Ohio and tallied almost with my appearance, tall one eye, black hair mine was light....I finished dinner and the man asked me, in writing, if I would allow my baggage to be examined. This caused me to laugh outright for it told me the suspicion was more than I had thought. I arose, beckoned to the bully, a doctor. He followed, some of the crowd also, upstairs to my room. The landlord came in also and sat quietly as though regretting the affair. I pulled forward a couple of trunks and handed my bunch of keys to the doctor. He motioned to the trunks and I understood and laid them open, also a carpet bag. One of the trunks was full of books. Doctor did nothing, so I opened two or three and showed my name and former residences. Clothing also with my name. Also on the brass handle of my umbrella. Crowd began to thin out again. The doctor reflected a moment, jumped up and went out. The landlord then wrote that it was all the work of the post office clerks, and asked me to pass it over as a mistake. I may add my name did not correspond with that in the handbill and that, meeting the doctor afterwards, I told him my hair was not black. His reply was "Hair can be colored." At Galena, the stage wagon carrying the mails, started. I was in it with four or five men. At dusk, we reached the Mississippi opposite Dubuque, Iowa. There was a sort of shanty made of boards nailed perpendicular; open door, no windows or fire place and no sign of being inhabited. The men sent a hail across, and after a half hour a large skiff came over rowed by one man. We all entered with the mail bags, and arrived in Dubuque. We stopped at Tim Fanning's tavern. Tim was a tall, lanky, good natured Irishman. His was the only hotel in town. Being a double log cabin, that is, twice the usual length, and two stories high, it had sufficient accommodations for the travel of that day.

The next morning, I inquired of Tim Fanning for George H. Walworth, whose acquaintance I had made in Hartford, Conneticut. Tim referred me to Timothy Davis, a lawyer. Found Davis in a small shanty of an office. Davis informed me that Walworth and he were partners and that the former was at the Buffalo Forks of the Wapsipinicon, forty miles out from Dubuque, and was building mills. This was a poser for the moment. My letters from the Walworths had always been dated Dubuque, and now I *found they were forty miles out in the wilderness. Davis however was a shrewd and kindly man and told me he had a horse he wished to send to Walworth and that I could take it the next day. In the course of the day, he came to Fanning's hotel where I was informed that two men would start for Iowa City next morning via the Buffalo Forks and that I could accompany them. Dubuque was then a straggling village, one or two two-story buildings, and a few smaller of frame or logs. The next morning, I was at Davis's office. Two men, mounted on ponies, apparently not much larger than good sized donkeys, stopped there. Davis's boy had a horse saddled and ready. The road was only a wagon track through the grass. Alongside was a single furrow plowed and at every mile or so a mound of sod about four feet high.*

*My fellow travelers: the name of one was Barlett, a merchant in Dubuque and a man of intelligence; the other was younger and a blacksmith. They rode ponies which went at a slow trot. The horse I was on was large and took longer steps. This compelled me to walk him, and I soon fell behind a quarter or half mile, then putting the horse to a trot came up very easily. This continued till about noon where we came to a log dwelling, stopped and got dinner. Only a woman was in the house. Paid her a half dollar each and went on two miles and reached the north fork of the Maquoketa. Here was a new frame hotel nearly finished, and another house, owned by a Kentuckian named Delong. These and the log house where we took dinner were all the signs of civilization we had seen since leaving Dubuque that morning. The place was then, and has since borne the name of Cascade...*

*About noon, we passed the first broken or plowed prairie we had seen on the route of forty miles. Crossing the hill on which the Roswell Crane building now stands, we were on what has since become Anamosa. We saw a tall, heavy man coming up the road. My companions stopped and questioned him. I was some way behind as usual. Reaching them they motioned me to turn off to the right when we came to where the road forked. We parted, they for Iowa City to attend the first sale of town lots. Turning my horse into the road on the right, I rode through the low bushes and kept on, whither I could only guess. Saw on the right of the road a piece of four or five acres broken by the plow and unfenced. Further on descried a log cabin in the distance about a mile ahead. Along my left was Buffalo Creek. Nearing the cabin, I turned the horse's head to the south side but he seemed to insist going on the north. Let him have his way and stopped in front of the only door to the house.*

*Nobody was around. But Emily Walworth, in the house, saw and recognized me, ran out, shook hands, then around the corner beckoning me to follow. There stood a carriage at rest and her sister Mary Ann in it, reading. The men were all lounging around at the newly raised mill. These men, seeing a horse and rider, came up to the place and I had an old friend's welcome from George, Caleb and John Denison Walworth. Reaching the end of the journey with not five dollars in pocket and seventy in Mobley's Bank in Dubuque, my first object was some kind of work. Having passed my boyhood on a farm, I had no fears regarding success.*

*At the mills, as the place was called, on the Buffalo, now Fisherville and two miles or so from Anamosa, there were, through the summer (1839), about eighteen men and two girls already mentioned. The men engaged in building a dam and sawmill, and the girls in housework, cooking and washing. Some of them had families living on the prairies, as the country south of the timber was called. I engaged with the owner of the place to work at 75 cents per day and board. It was regarded as pretty good wages at the time."*

This next bit of information about Edmund Booth and Mary Ann Walworth comes from Volume One - *History Of Jones County Past and Present.* (15)

The first marriage license issued in Jones county was granted to Edmund Booth and Mary Ann Walworth, July 25, 1840 and on the following day, they were married by the Justice John G. Joslin. This is the first marriage that appears on the record of the clerk's office at Anamosa at the present time....the procuring of this license also hangs a tale. Mr. Booth went to the clerk's house to get a permit, as it was termed, to be married. The clerk was not home and as he had no office other than his cabin and residence, this was naturally the place where he would be expected to be found. Mr. Booth was told that the clerk was cradling wheat about two miles north of Cascade. Nothing daunted, Mr. Booth set out on foot in search for the clerk who was found working for a man named Brown. When Mr. Booth got there, neither of them had any pen or pencil or paper to write out the permit. Printed forms were not then in use in the clerk's office. Mr. Booth and Mr. Clark then returned to Cascade where the permit was written and signed. With a lighter heart, Mr. Booth trudged his way homeward and on July 25, 1840. The first marriage ceremony in the county was performed under the authority of a Jones County license.

[Author's note as of 2009- without knowing the exact location of Mr.

Brown's farm north of Cascade - that could have been as much as 20 miles one way on foot from Anamosa, he would probably have taken Military Road both ways - remember this is 1840].

Back to the present. Tonight I'm staying in Anamosa at Casey and Christina Ditch's home. I had roofed their home earlier this summer and they'd graciously offered to let me spend the night. We have a pizza party and watch the KWWL TV interview taken earlier that morning in Martelle. I have another great night's sleep.

---

# 4

# Anamosa To Monticello

## September 11, 2008

I get an early start. Today promises to be another big day. We'd hoped to take the Kirkwood Alternative High School students out to Eleanor Jacob's farm east of Langworthy to see the only remaining portion of the original road bed still in existence as far as I know. The ground is too muddy, however and it is decided I would meet the students in their classroom. Tonight I get to sleep in my own bed...but first I have to get there.

The route I've chosen takes me past what is now J&P Cycle. It is an older portion of Highway 151. Like much of my chosen route, wherever the older road still exists, I walk that rather than today's four lane highway. At the top of the hill, before getting back onto today's road, I look back to Anamosa, taking some pictures. It is overcast. The hillsides are still heavily timbered. I can easily imagine what this would have looked like 160 years ago.

I'm making good time as I pass mile marker 59 and a sign on my right for the village of Scotch Grove. Scotch Grove (originally called Applegate's Crossing) is seven miles to the east.

## John Lovejoy

This seems like the perfect spot to tell you about John Lovejoy. My initial curiosity about him was because of his last name...Lovejoy. The more I learned, however, the more his story drew me in.

John Lovejoy was a farmer, postmaster, choir director at the Scotch Grove Presbyterian Church, railroad station agent, and ambassador to Peru under Lincoln. For a very short time, part owner of a local newspaper with Edmund Booth that eventually became the *Anamosa Eureka*.

John Ellingwood Lovejoy was born October 13, 1817 in Albion, Kennebec County, Maine. He came from a line of pastors. His father, Daniel, was a circuit riding preacher, which explains the strong spiritual thread that ran through his life. He was the youngest of nine children. In 1835 he went to St. Louis, where he learned the printer's trade working for his brother Elijah P. Lovejoy. In 1837, his brother is killed by a pro slavery mob in Alton, Illinois because of his stand against slavery. The unrest leading up to the Civil War was taking place twenty six years before the start of the Civil War.

In December of 1839, John moved to Scotch Grove, Iowa, where he eventually met and married another settler's daughter, Margaret Living-ston. Margaret was born November 23, 1823. Her family was part of the Scottish migration from the Selkirk Settlement in Red River, Manitoba.

John and Margaret eventually have five children. In 1861, John was appointed U.S. Ambassador to Peru, a position he held for about three and a half years. Margaret died April 15, 1869, before John was able to return home. In 1871, he married Joanna Macbeth. She was 26, he 54. They go on to have two children of their own. He continued to farm, and then opened a mercantile business in Center Junction. In 1875, he became the station agent for the Chicago, Milwaukee & St. Paul Railroad in Scotch Grove.

John Lovejoy dies June 5, 1891 at the age of 73. (16)

Here is another historical sketch about John Lovejoy I found in a book given to me by Michelle Shover: (17)

*John E. Lovejoy was a large man whose presence would be felt no matter how large the company. His full black beard, his dark piercing eyes and his firm, steady step spoke more than words could ever express that he had a fine mind and clear vision....*

*Lovejoy was an active and resourceful person. He had learned telegra-phy as a hobby when a boy. He was the agent for the railroad company in our small country village, Scotch Grove, and lived in the country a short distance from our home and a mile and a half from the depot. It was my job to deliver the milk from our small herd of cows to the creamery at the station each morning and evening. Daily for a number of years, Mr. Love-joy timed his going to work that he might ride with me. He was a silent man. His was a reticence that I had not seen in any man before him and have not known in anyone since he passed from out of my view. Tennyson has well described him as he portrays so much that is fine and superb in life, "Such fine reserve and noble reticence." I cannot remember that in all those rides he spoke a word save as he gave a brief reply to some petty question I may have asked when the silence and the monotony of the mo-*

ments could no longer be endured. It is strange how loud is the tromp of horse's hooves and the crunch of the wagon wheels when two persons ride together without conversation.

For a short time, Lovejoy was in partnership with Edmund Booth in Anamosa with regard to the local newspaper. Lovejoy's personal friend, President Lincoln, had appointed him to the important post of Minister to Peru. He took up his work with courage...but there was bad news from home. His sons or some of them could not adjust their rural life with the atmosphere that an important office had created for the head of the family. They neglected their work. In the spirit of show when in company it was said they would light their pipes with dollar bills. The salary of a minister of the U.S. to a foreign country could not long stand this strain. And there were other troubles that weighed heavily. His wife (Margaret Livingston), was wasting rapidly from tuberculosis. He was needed at home. Mr. Lovejoy wrote the State Department at Washington urgently for leave of absence....but there was no answer...weeks slipped by. Word from home was most discouraging; "the wife would not linger long.."

## The early Scottish families that settled in Scotch Grove

In 1837 five Scottish families walked thirteen hundred miles from the Red River Settlement in Manitoba to the newly opened Black Hawk Territory. They traveled on foot and with large two wheeled carts called the Pembina cart.

Here is a description of their cart taken from the 1937 Centennial booklet on Scotch Grove: (18)

"The Red River or Pembina cart, was the vehicle used for this thousand mile journey. This was a product of the locality, doubtless of French origin, and handed down to the Bois Brules or half-breeds by their French ancestors. For seventy-five years it was the freight car and family carriage of the community. The only tools needed to make the cart were an axe to cut down a tree and a gun to shoot an elk or buffalo. Two huge wooden wheels over five feet in diameter with eleven or twelve spokes set into a wooden hub seemed the most essential feature. The body was made of rough boards laid lengthwise and pegged down by one crosswise board pegged to the axle. A rude framework several feet high to be covered by a buffalo skin completed the body. The shafts were an extension of a board *in the body with a hole bored about a foot from the end, to which the harness holding the ox drawing the cart was attached.*

*Scottish pioneers and their two wheeled Ox cart (19)*

*This was the Red River cart which carried these Scotch Grove pioneers and their belongings in a thousand mile journey over nightmarish roads or no roads at all. In sloughs or deep mud holes the long spokes enabled the wheels to reach solid ground. When they had to cross deep streams, they lashed the wheels together to form a raft for the body, the men and animals swimming the current. There were no luxurious springs to tempt even the most tired travelers with promises of easy riding, and its approach was heralded for miles by the screech of the wooden axles.*

*With these carts loaded with from seven hundred to a thousand pounds and followed by whatever livestock they owned, these pioneers traveled southward through that summer of 1837. Burning sun, violent hailstorms, wind and rain beat upon them in turn as they plodded on; mosquitoes and flies tormented them; fear of wandering Indians harassed them. At night, the carts became their fortress as hub to hub they were placed in a circle, while within this rude stockade the travelers cooked, ate, and slept, always guarded by one of their number. The story goes that their hired guide became insane or at least very unreliable and caused them many anxious days and nights....*

*They came down the west side of the Mississippi River to Dubuque and then pushed on across the Maquoketa River to the edge of the native timber. Here, after four months of travel, they felt they had found an abiding place."*

# Langworthy and the Wade Family Tragedy

As you near mile marker 60, you'll see the sign for Langworthy. You'll want to turn left off of Highway 151 at this point and get on the old highway. What's left of the town of Langworthy will be on your left. There are two families I want to tell you about as you pass Langworthy; the Monk and the Wade families.

My grandpa, John Monk (we called him Opa which is low German for grandpa), grew up two miles west of Langworthy. Like I mentioned in the beginning of this book, this whole adventure started because of him. Grandpa was one of six boys and six girls.

Grandpa used to talk about a train wreck he remembered south of Langworthy in the dead of winter.

*Grandpa Monk's family. He is top, left.*

Grandpa told me the engineer had tried to buck some big snow drifts and had derailed the engine, and became pinned in the wreckage. Grandpa remembered hearing a doctor hollering "Get some whiskey, get some whiskey" for the trapped engineer. Here is the account of the accident from the Monticello Express dated January 17, 1929:

The Monticello Express, January 17, 1929.
Train Wrecked at Langworthy Friday Noon.

*"Roscoe Stevens suffers a fractured leg. Earl Delay, thumb.*

*Three trainmen were injured, two miles south of Langworthy, Friday noon. Roscoe Stevens, of Marion, was pinned under a wrecked locomotive for more than three hours and suffered the compound fracture of one of his legs. Both legs were badly burned by hot steam. Mr. Stevens suffered seriously from shock and exposure in addition to his other injuries. It was necessary to use a large jack to raise the locomotive sufficiently to get him out. His injured leg has been put into a cast and Dr. Redmond, the attending physician, is confident that he will save the leg. Stevens was the second engineer on the second locomotive of the doubleheader.*

*Two other men were injured: L. J. Burrows, Marion, engineer on the first locomotive of the double header, who suffered a badly wrenched back and internal injuries on the same locomotive and Earl Daley, the fireman on the same engine, suffered a compound fracture of his right thumb. Henry Dersch, a traveling engineer, riding on the same engine, suffered a number of bruises. Bill Loutz, fireman of the second engine, escaped with a few scratches.*

*The accident apparently resulted when the train, consisting of a double header engine, mail car, and coach van, ran into a heavy snow drift. The train left Cedar Rapids at 8 o'clock Friday morning and was stalled at various times until it steamed out of Anamosa at noon. The derailment oc-curred when the front engine jumped the track when hitting an unusually heavy drift. Both engines were thrown to the left side of the track. Engine number one ran up the side of the bank and then turned turtle. When it stopped, the steam was still on and the wheels turning. The baggage coach broke loose from the second engine and was tipped over on its side. The*

*passenger coach was derailed but did not overturn. Two Monticello men enjoyed the thrills of the wreck: viz: Fred S. Stuhler and X. Ray Childress. The latter came near freezing his foot while working to free Stevens who was pinned underneath the locomotive.*

*A wrecker from Savannah appeared on the scene Saturday morning and the entire wreck was cleaned up by Sunday. Trains detoured by way of Oxford Junction. Saturday, Mrs. Roscoe Stevens is with her husband at the McDonald Hospital and Mrs. Leonard Burrows, and two daughters, visited during the early part of the week with Mr. Burrows who is still at the hospital. It was impossible to set Mr. Stevens fractured leg until Monday afternoon on account of the swelling. Dr. T. M. Redmond, the local physician for the C. M. St. Paul & Pacific Railway, reports that all men are out of danger and on the road to recovery.*

Clarence Heyen

*Clarence Heyen*

*Early Delay will be laid up for two months with his injured right hand and Roscoe Stevens will, of course, take a longer enforced vacation due to the fact that his injuries are more serious. Mr. Burrows' injuries are such that Dr. Redmond has been unable to estimate how long he will be laid up. This was the most serious wreck that has occurred near Monticello in a good many years."*

I (Doug), think my favorite story took place when Grandpa was in his late teens or early 20s. He was collecting money for the Wayne Lutheran Church. He was a big strapping farm boy, six foot two, 240 pounds, quiet and shy. He stopped by Clarence Heyen's general store to collect money for the Wayne Lutheran Church.

There were five or six young men from Monticello hanging around because there was a dance later that night. Grandpa told me during those days, some people didn't like the Germans. As he walked into the store, he said "How are you guys?" One of the boys said, "What's it to you?"

*Marie Otten (second from right) coming to America on a ship.*

IMMIGRANTS—1929 STYLE

MARIE OTTEN.          ALMUTH KRELLE.

We don't exactly understand Mr. Hoover's stand on the immigration question but if his plan would exclude from the United States such comely young German girls as these, we hope congress turns thumbs down on the proposal. These girls, Almuth Krelle and Marie Otten, arrived in Wayne township, Jones county, a few days ago from Bremerhaven, Germany. They couldn't speak English but by their dress no one could distinguish them from girls who had spent all their lives in America. They wear their hair bobbed, and their skirts short, and their frocks are of the latest mode. They are relatives of the Otto Otten and Fred Otten families of Wayne and Scotch Grove townships. They plan to make their home in this country and are preparing to go to work like most energetic American girls now are doing.

*Newspaper clipping*
*of my grandma and a friend*

A few minutes later as John stepped back outside, someone hit him from behind and knocked him to the ground, then they all piled onto him. Grandpa thought to himself they were after the church money he was carrying. He was able to get back on his feet and start swinging. What those boys didn't reckon with was Grandpa was one of six boys who loved to fight and wrestle. He said by the time he was finished, the last one had run to the car and was crying like a little baby.

The following Monday, Grandpa was at a local farm to buy hogs for his dad (Henry Monk)...when the son of the farmer came out of the house, he had a big red hand print on the side of his face, compliments of Grandpa. Grandpa told the father he was sorry about it. The dad told Grandpa, not to worry - the kid had it coming.

My Oma (grandmother) Marie Otten, immigrated from Germany in 1929.

*Grandma Marie visiting her Uncle Fred and Aunt Hannah Otten*
*Scotch Grove, Iowa*

The newspaper clipping read as follows:

*"We don't exactly understand Mr. Hoover's stand on the immigration question but if his plan would exclude from the United States such comely young German girls as these, we hope congress turns thumbs down on the proposal. These girls, Almuth Krelle and Marie Otten, arrived in Wayne Township, Jones County, few days ago from Bremerhaven, Germany. They couldn't speak English but by their dress, no one could distinguish them from girls who had spent all their lives in America. They wear their hair bobbed, and their skirts short, and their frocks are of the latest mode. They are relatives of the Otto Otten and Fred Otten families of Wayne and Scotch Grove townships. They plan to make their home in this country and are preparing to work like most energetic American girls are now doing."*

The way I understand it, while Grandma was visiting her Aunt and Uncle Otten, the family got together with Grandpa Monk's family to play cards which is where they first met.

Together, they had three children, Don (my dad), Roserithia (Rosie), and John. I can still remember growing up, listening to the adults speaking German around the kitchen table.

One of the stories that caught my ear had to do with making moonshine during the Prohibition. These are the details that I remember. Grandpa and his brother Mano for sure were in on it. I remember grandpa talking about the still being hidden in one of the hog feeders. Not only did they make moonshine for themselves but they had a delivery route that went up through Worthington, Iowa.

Here is the moonshine recipe given to me by my grandfather:

*"You take a hundred pounds of sugar, a bushel of rye. Let it soak for a week. Put it on the stove, bring it to a boil. In the lid, you have a hole to let the steam out. Attach a coil of tube to the hole. Put the end of the tube in the jug. That's all there is to it."*

After you pass Langworthy, you'll go a quarter of a mile and see a gravel road marked "Military Road." As you go north on this gravel road, as of this writing, Eleanor Jacobs lives on the first farm you pass on the right. Before my walk, we stopped and visited with Eleanor. She told us the original portion of Military Road was still visible in her pasture, and we were welcome to look at it.

The road bed in the pasture runs north and south. As it goes south, the original stone work of a bridge that crossed Kitty Creek is still visible. Eleanor told us a story about a family and one of their children who had died on this portion of the road, having been caught in a snow storm. This was the same story Joy Adams had told us previously.

As I walk north on the gravel, I think to myself, this is the very area where that tragedy played out over 150 years ago. I could not imagine that dad frantically battling for the life of his wife and small child.....

Here are two accounts of that tragic event, the first coming from *The History of Jones County* Volume 1. (21)

From the personal reminiscences of the early days of Monticello by Mrs. Martha J. Gallagher:

*"I think it was the winter of 1856-57 that we had the big blizzard. Sunday morning was fair and warm for the time of year. The day turned out to be beautiful until about 4 o'clock in the afternoon. Nearly everyone that didn't have company went somewhere. We went to a neighbor's that day, but got home just as the storm broke in its fury. It was all my father could do to get from the stable to the house. On what is now the Hosford farm on the main road lived an Englishman by the name of Wade. The farm was then owned by Mr. Walworth. They were our neighbors to the south. They had a family of ten children, the eldest a boy of 19 and the youngest about a year old. In the morning the father and mother drove out near Lang-*

worthy, taking the baby with them to a Mr. Schriven's to spend the day and also bring back one of the daughters home with them to do some sewing. They started back when the sun was yet shining. The storm came up so suddenly that in a few minutes, it was impossible to see anything before them. Before they reached home they lost their way. The horses wouldn't face the storm. They drove around and round within a short distance of home until the horses gave out. Then Mr. Wade unhitched the team and spread some quilts down under some willows not far from where Alonzo Hosford used to live. The woman and the baby got on them and he spread more over them. Then as we supposed, he started on foot to try to find some place. It wasn't very cold until toward morning, then it turned bitter cold with the wind still blowing.

Just as we were getting up the next morning, the eldest son came. My father said," What brings you so early such a cold morning?" Then he said his father and mother went away the day before and had not returned yet, and he was afraid they had been lost in the storm. He wanted my father to go with him to look for them. We told him perhaps they had never started home. My father suggested that he go home and get the children up and as soon as we could get some breakfast and get the chores done, we would come up and see what could be done. We notified some of the neighbors and they in turn told others until all were informed. My father first drove out to the Schriven's to see if they were there. Then as the news of their real loss spread, all the men and boys too who were large enough went to look for them. The snow had covered their tracks except on some high places. They hunted all day and all night and the next day until about noon before they found any trace of them. Someone saw the corner of one of the quilts sticking out of the snow, and there they found the woman and the baby. Then they hunted until near night before they found Wade. He had walked and probably hallooed until he fell dead.

They brought them to our house, and we had to lay them around the stove to thaw out so as to get their clothes off. My mother and some others of the neighbors stayed with the children all the time until after the funeral. They found the horses just where he had unhitched them. They had not moved out of their tracks. It took hard work to get them to the house. They lived, but were not able to do anything the rest of the winter. This happened two weeks before Christmas. Wades had planned to have a big dinner on Christmas and invited several of the neighbors. They had their turkey killed and hung up to freeze. So on Christmas, all the neighbors that were expecting to be there, baked up all sorts of good things and took them there, and cooked the turkey and had all the children sit down and *eat together for the last time as they had to be separated. All the neighbors that could took a child to keep until they could do better. One of the smaller ones lived with us several years. I should have said that the men got together and appraised the stock and household goods and made an auction. And after the funeral expenses were paid, divided the balance among the children. There were no legal proceedings, and no one charged anything for their services although some spent days attending to it."*

Back to the present.

It is on this stretch of the road that Jeremy, from the *Dubuque Telegraph Herald,* catches up with me, does a brief interview for the paper and takes some video footage of me walking. As I get to the end of the gravel road, I turn right on what we call the "Lower Prairieburg Road." This takes me into Monticello by the local John Deere implement store. I stop at Hardee's to have lunch with my parents and a few well-wishers before heading up to Hannah Byrne's Kirkwood alternative High School class to give them a brief presentation.

I've made t-shirts to commemorate my walk and give one to Hannah before I leave.

We have no idea what this area would have looked like to the first settlers.

Listen to this description of Kitty Creek by Martha J. Gallagher: (22)

*"The Kitty Creek of today is nothing as it was then. It was a beautiful stream; the water was as clear as crystal, with a gravelly bottom of pretty colored stones. It was so clear that you could see the bottom where it was several feet deep. I felt so disappointed the last time I saw it. The first time I saw it the upper falls had a fall of several feet and the water was churned into a white foam as it fell over the falls. The upper falls are above the bridge; I don't know as the lower falls show at all now."*

After leaving Kirkwood, I walk north getting ready to head out of Monticello.

Daniel Varvel's cabin would have been near here. Daniel Varvel came to Monticello in 1836 with William Clark from Kentucky as a single young man. He'd worked in the lead mines of Dubuque before building a claim cabin on the bank of the South Fork of the Maquoketa River. Listen to this description of early Monticello: (23)

*"The scene spread out before the sturdy pioneer was one of unsurpass-*

*ing loveliness. It was that of a fertile wilderness,...beauty and pregnant with promise. The wide prairies stretching in airy undulations far away, their sunny ridges and fertile slopes glowing beneath the brilliancy of the autumn sky, the beautiful Maquoketa and the smaller, but not less beautiful Kitty Creek, gliding beneath the overshadowing bluffs, and bordered with forests, upon the foliage of which the early frosts had spilled their golden stain. It was as the Garden of Eden lapsed into primeval wilderness and solitude, with no man to till the soil.....those times that tried men's souls are, for the most part, passed away...."*

*"By the time the winter had set in, Varvel and Clark were comfortably lodged for the season in a log cabin, prepared to bid defiance to tempest and frost, to savage and wild beast. The entire winter was spent in lonely and monotonous seclusion; but as both were experienced and ardent hunters and game plentiful...."*

Three years later (1839), Varvel's cabin would play host to the road crew building Old Military Road, and Edmund Booth among others.

Booth described his first glimpse of Varvel's cabin as he made his way from Dubuque to Buffalo Forks (Anamosa): (24)

*"As before said, the Military Road was being laid out, Congress having appropriated twenty thousand dollars. We found a newly broken furrow along one side of the road, which by the way was merely a track through the grass of the prairies, and a mound of turf raised three or four feet high at intervals of a half mile more or less....."*

*"Passing through the timber, the new road being pretty good, the light from the chinks of a log cabin at last gave us assurance of human habitation, and a chance for a night's lodging. It proved to be the dwelling of Daniel Varvel, situated on the south fork of the Maquoketa, and where is now a portion of the town of Monticello. ...In the house were some dozen or fifteen men, in the employ of the U.S. government contractor, and engaged in the laying out of the Military Road. They had come thus far with the work. Varvel prepared supper. He was at that time wifeless, and no woman in the house. Supper of ham and eggs, corn dodgers and coffee. Breakfast, ditto, and the next morning, eaten with a hearty relish after such a long ride."*

Here is the recipe for corn dodgers from *The American Cookbook* (25) that Joy Adams shared with me:

*"Mix with cold water into a soft dough one quart of southern corn meal*

*-sifted, a teaspoonful of salt, a tablespoonful of butter or lard, melted.*
*Mold into oval cakes with the hands and bake in a very hot oven, in well-*
*greased pans to be eaten hot. The crust should be brown."*

Hospitality- the word literally means "the lover of strangers." There is so much about this brief account I continue to think about.

I can't imagine cooking dinner for fifteen road workers plus three other visitors (Booth and his two traveling companions) over a wood stove... that was a lot of food to prepare.

Secondly, this food was coming out of his personal provisions....that would represent three weeks of meals for himself...in other words, he (Varvel), was not living from week to week in terms of provisions.

Thirdly, there were not a lot of places to stay at this point in history, so if a traveler showed up at your door, then you took care of him...period.

I realize it's a very small detail, but to change corn dodgers to "wheat bread" is not a small detail....wheat did not grow well in this area, Indian corn was the staple of the day.

As I've begun to attempt to be more self-sufficient (food wise), one of the foods I have decided to grow is corn (not the newly genetic modified stuff), but an heirloom variety that the locals would have grown 150 years ago. Studying that menu means Varvel must have had a few chickens and pigs at his cabin as well.

I cross the Maquoketa River bridge, walk through what used to be called "East Monticello" on the old maps and spend the night at our home which is only ½ mile off of Highway 151.

*Picture of our house the morning I leave for Cascade.*

# 5

# Monticello

# to North of Cascade

September 12, 2008

I leave home around 7 a.m., day 5 of my walk. I feel like Frodo Baggins (from the Lord of the Rings movie), leaving home. I take a picture of our bed and breakfast house. I have so much to be thankful for. Micaela and Joy plan to meet me for lunch in Cascade. Today I will swing by the Cascade Protestant Cemetery and pay my respects to Lyman Dillon. But I'm getting ahead of myself....two miles east of our home on Old Military Road, is the Bowens Prairie Cemetery, all that remains of another early settlement.

Bowens Prairie was once situated on the edge of another large timber. At one point, it was the home of two churches, the *Palmer Cheese Factory*, a school and several families. When the railroad decided to bypass the community in the 1870s, that more or less was the final nail in the coffin. To give you an idea of just how thriving the community was at one point, one of the local churches boasted a sixty member choir.

## Bowens Prairie and Alfred Denson

Alison Krauss sings a song called "Jacob's Dream." It's a sad song about two little boys who wander away from their mom in 1856 and perish. If you get a chance, listen to the song. It's a powerful backdrop to the true story I'm going to share with you next. I found it originally in *The History Of Jones County 1879* (26)

Here are the lyrics to the Alison Krauss song:

*"In the spring of 1856 with the snow still on the ground*
*Two little boys were lost in the mountains above the town*
*The father went out hunting, the boys had stayed behind*
*While mother tended to her chores, they wandered from her side*
*The two had gone to follow him and lost their way instead*
*By dusk the boys had not been found and fear had turned to dread.*
*200 men had gathered there to comb the mountain side*
*The fires were built on the highest peak in hopes they'd see the light.*

*Oh mommy and daddy why can't you hear our cries*
*The day is almost over, soon it will be night*
*We're so cold and hungry and our feet are tired and sore*
*We promise not to stray again from our cabin door*

*Now Jacob Diverd woke one night from a strange and eerie dream*
*He saw a path between two hills near a dark and swollen stream*
*He told his wife he saw the boys huddled close beside a log*
*For two more nights the dream returned this vision sent from God*

*Oh mommy and daddy why can't you hear our cries*
*The day is almost over, soon it will be night*
*We're so cold and hungry and our feet are tired and sore*
*We promise not to stray again from our cabin door*

*a thousand men had searched in vain the west side of pop's creek*
*But Jacob's wife knew of this place and said to travel east*
*With a guide to take him there, Jacob came upon the scene*
*And found the boys cold and still beneath the old birch tree*

*Oh mommy and daddy, look past the tears you cry*
*We're both up in Heaven now, God is by our side*
*As you lay us down to rest in the presence of the Lord*
*Know that we will meet you here at Heaven's door*

*Oh mommy and daddy, look past the tears you cry*
*We're both up in Heaven now, God is by our side*
*And as you lay us down to rest in the presence of the Lord*
*Know that we will meet you here at Heaven's door."*

- Alison Krauss

Here is the account of Alfred Denson. This took place just two miles east of where I currently live in the town of Bowen's Prairie: (27)

*"On the 24th of April, following a most melancholy event transpired on the prairie, filling the whole community with gloom, and the family immediately interested, with unspeakable anguish. The circumstances were these:*

*We had finished our out-door work and chores, glad to enter the house to sit down and enjoy the cheerful fire blazing upon the hearth, which the cold, bleak Northeast wind and rain rendered peculiarly grateful to our chilled bodies. Darkness had set in, rendering the out-door desolation doubly so. Suddenly we were aroused by a knock at the door, and the entrance of two of our neighbors, who informed us that a boy was lost. Alfred Denson, a remarkable bright and amiable lad of six years, and the light of the household had wandered from the house and was lost, either on the cold bleak prairie, or in the still more dismal forest. The instant the information was communicated, we felt that the poor boy's fate was sealed. If he had wandered into the thick woods, he might possibly survive until morning, but if, as we feared, he had strayed out into the wide, unprotected prairie, we felt that his sleep that night would be ("the sleep from which there is no awakening").*

*Dark and dreary and uncomfortable as was the night, the citizens were aroused, and started out with the resolution to do what they could. But the night was intensely dark; we were destitute of lanterns and were obliged to depend on torches to guide us in our travels, and these were comparatively useless on account of the strong wind and rain. We expected to get lost ourselves, but this did not deter us. Our first design was to search the forest in the vicinity of the child's home, and build fires in different places, if possible, the child might discover some of them; they also might be guiding stars to the searchers.*

*There was a timber road leading into the forest which we thought possibly the boy might have taken, and examining it particularly with the light of our torches, we discovered his track leading into the forest. This encouraged us to proceed, thinking now we had ascertained the direction he had taken. We were also the more encouraged in regard to the safety of the boy as if we should not find him that night, he might obtain a shelter which would save him from perishing. Soon, however, we found another track of his retracing steps, and leading back into the prairie. On this discovery, we were thrown into confusion in regard to the course we should take. We knew not whether he would abide by the road, and thus reach the open* prairie, or whether in the darkness, he might have left it and still wandering in the forest. We, however, followed it and again discovered his track near the Northeast corner of Hugh Bowen's field, and some 100 rods out, into the open prairie. Here, we took rails from the fence and built a large fire which could be seen all through the settlement. We built the fire also, partly, as guide to the child if he should be fortunate enough to see it, and partly as a pilot to ourselves.

Hoping that possibly he might, in his wanderings, have reached some of the neighbors, we visited those living on the north side of the prairie, to wit: Moses Collins, Charles Johnston and Franklin Dalby. Not discovering any further trace of the child, we proceeded thence westerly on a neighborhood road, became bewildered, losing our track and course. We then commenced shouting, and obtained a response from the elder Mr. Dalby. We groped our way to his residence, and deeming it advisable to hunt no further before daylight, we encamped by the fire for the night.

For two succeeding days, the whole community including Cascade and Monticello, comprising some thirty persons, made a systematic search through the timber, north and south of the settlement, and the prairie between but without success, and it was not until the fourth day afterward that the lifeless body of the boy was discovered nearly covered up with the tall slough-grass, some eighty rods north of the present residence of T.W. Little and nearly two miles distant from his home. He doubtless perished on the first night of his wanderings. The sympathizing neighbors immediately collected and assisted as best they could in performing the last rites of burial. There was no minister to officiate. The little band of sincere mourners bore the child to its last resting place, there to rest in peace until the resurrection morn. And this marks the era of the first death and burial on Bowen's Prairie."

Grave marker for Alfred Denson at Bowen Praire Cemetery placed by Bill Corbin, local historian from Monticello.

# Chance encounter with Pam Foley
## and her dad's research on Lyman Dillon

One of the serendipitous encounters I had this past year as I was re-searching the Military Road and Lyman Dillon, was a conversation with Pam Foley from Monticello. She owns an antique store called Weekend Antiques. I asked her if she had any old history books for sale? She told me her dad, Gus Norlin, had been researching Lyman Dillon and Old Military Road before he passed away but never published his research. Gus was the former president of *The Jones County Historical Society*. Pam offered to let me look through her dad's research.

Here is a portion from a newspaper clipping dated 1928: (28)

*"Lyman Dillon was born near Utica, New York, June 1, 1800. He and a younger brother were left orphans at a tender age. In those days, they did not say adopted but 'bound out.' The younger of these boys was 'bound out' to a minister. He grew to young manhood studying the minis-try and died when quite young. Lyman Dillon was 'bound out' to a tavern keeper who worked him very hard. He had a great desire for education but had little opportunity. Books and even newspapers were scarce then. He would get what he could from travelers stopping at the tavern. They helped and encouraged him. He finally ran away and went to Utica, New York. Working and going to school until he graduated from a college in Utica. He then followed Greeley's well known admonition and "went west." He bought a tract of land from the government near Cascade, Iowa and erected a saw mill. He was known among the early settlers as a man who was "generous to a fault."*

*An instance of this is noted in his action when a poor family arrived in the community from Germany. The parents were sick upon arriving at Dubuque and had no way of continuing the journey to Cascade with four children. Dillon, hearing their predicament, went to Dubuque and brought them to Cascade. The parents were unable to sit up, but a mattress was provided and upon this they lay while making the trip. Dillon provided a little home for them, but they were never able to work. Mrs. Dillon took the little children into her home and cared for them. The parents continued ill and one day shortly before their death..."* Article is cut off at this point.

Here is Irvin Webber's material from Volume 4 – *History of Iowa City* (29):

"Way back in 1839, 147 years ago, Lyman Dillon plowed a furrow from Dubuque to Iowa City. Reportedly it is the longest furrow ever plowed- almost 100 miles. Using a prairie breaking plow and five, slow, lumbering, stubborn oxen, he completed the contract for the U.S. Government.

According to an old legend, Iowa City merchants, in 1839, had hired Lyman Dillon, who lived in Cascade (15 miles from Dubuque), to plow a furrow from Iowa City to Dubuque to guide pioneers and settlers through the hilly, heavily timbered country to Iowa City, the newly selected capital of the Territory of Iowa.

Actually, at the time, the U.S. Government was fostering the construction of military roads on the western frontier, and on March 4, 1839, Congress appropriated $20,000 for a road to run from Dubuque to Iowa City, and then later to be extended to the northern boundary of Missouri, near present Keosauqua.

That road today is the diagonal paved road Highways 1 and 151, from Iowa City to Dubuque via Solon, Ivanhoe (Cedar River), Mount Vernon, Anamosa, Monticello and Cascade. As always happens with new roads, towns sprang up wherever a major river was met- Ivanhoe, Anamosa, Monticello and Cascade.

The road from Dubuque to Iowa City was immediately surveyed with U.S. Army engineer Tilghman directing the work. He engaged Dillon to plow the furrow to guide the road builders. James, Lucious, and Edward Langworthy, three brothers who had been engaged in lead mining in Galena, Illinois as early as 1824, and, in 1839 in Dubuque, were given the contract to build the road as far as the Cedar River.

Dillon came from New York to the frontier in 1836 and settled in Cascade, where he operated a saw mill on the north fork of the Maquoketa River. He married the daughter of another pioneer from New York, who had settled in the Cascade area....

While there is disagreement as to whether Dillon started the furrow at Iowa City or Dubuque, more evidence points to its having been started at Tim Fanning's Log Cabin Tavern in Dubuque, and ending at Butler's Capital in Iowa City (Northeast corner of Clinton and Washington).

Both places are long since gone, but the Daughters of the American Revolution bronze plaque marking the start of the furrow is now on the wall of Torbert's Drug Store in Dubuque."

(Authors note: As I'm retyping this, *Lot One*, a bar, is now situated where Torbert's Drug Store was once located), a plaque marking the end, is at the parking lot of the First National Bank in Iowa City, once a stagecoach stop.

*"When Dillon and his party started their furrow in Dubuque, they were accompanied by a wagon with supplies for the trip, food, provisions, tents and blankets. At sundown, they pitched their tents, cooked their evening meal, and rolled up in their blankets and slept to be ready for the next day's grind at sunrise.*

*I had always wondered why oxen were used on the frontier rather than horses. But oxen could be driven day after day after day without rest, whereas horses had to be rested. An ox, if you are wondering as once was I, can be either a steer or a cow, usually the former, and is called an ox because it is trained as a beast of burden.*

*The military road, started as soon as Dillon had finished the furrow, was built primarily to enable the Dragoons, a military stationed in Dubuque, to reach the interior of the state quickly in case of an Indian uprising. There was concern the pioneers might move into Indian territory ahead of schedule or into territory not yet ceded to the government.*

*Fortunately, the situation never arose and the Dragoons were never called. Poweshiek and his Indians in Johnson County were peaceful, and friendly relation existed between the Indians and the early settlers. In fact, Poweshiek and his men came to the funeral of John Gilbert, a trader.*

*The military road cut a clean swath 40 feet wide through forests and bushes and grading through swamps. Contracts for bridges were supposed to have been made, but there is some question how soon they were completed, and fords and ferries were used at the onset.*

*While the military was not needed, the road proved to be of great help in guiding the prairie schooners, miners, immigrants, merchants and adventurers.*

*Once completed, the road served the four-horse stage coach for Iowa City, Dubuque and Galena, Illinois with Iowa City, the territorial capital, a hub for stagecoaches in all directions. Taverns in the new towns along the road served as overnight stops for the stages.*

*About 800 teams reportedly passed over the road in the early 1850s as prospectors from all parts of the nation were lured by the newly discovered gold fields in California. Some came as solitary units, others in large well organized parties of men with a few women. In those years, it was not uncommon to see large groups of California-bound covered wagons camped on the east bank of the Iowa River at Iowa Avenue, waiting their turn to be ferried. Their problems along the military road were minor to those encountered in Nebraska and further west where they were subject* to attacks by Indians....

Lyman Dillon died of cancer at the relatively young age of 57, not a
wealthy man, but one of the leaders among pioneers, and one sought
out for his counsel. But a monument to his name lives on in the 100 mile
furrow he plowed. The next time you speed along Highway 1 and 151, how
about a smile in memory of this Iowa pioneer."

# Cascade

One of the "discoveries" I've made this past year as I've researched
is that there are conflicting details surrounding virtually every detail of
Lyman Dillon and the furrow. Here is one principle to keep in mind as you
try to discover the facts: *The older the source, the more weight it carries.*

In the September 7, 1922 edition of the *Cascade Pioneer*, there is a col-
umn titled "*An Old, Old Pioneer Speaks*", written by Captain John O'Sullivan. Here is a portion of an article:

*"Cascade Iowa, August 30, 1922. To the Editor, I am the oldest mem-
ber living born in Jones. I will take the liberty of giving you a little of the
history of this end of the county at a time when I knew every man in the
county. My father, John O'Sullivan, came to Dubuque in the spring of 1836
and took up a claim one mile west of Ballaelough, but a man by the name
of James Regan, jumped the claim and so in the spring of 1837, he came
over into what afterwards became Richland Township in Jones County
and took up a claim in section three. He put up a house in the Northeast
corner of the Northwest quarter of section three where I was born October
19, 1840.*

*In 1838 my father drove a team of six yoke of cattle to lay out the Mili-
tary Road from Cascade to Iowa City. Charles Johnson had the contract.
The same year he helped William Moore to build his house.....*

*My father helped to build a log house on what is now the William
Aitchison farm and which used to be known as the Frank Hicks farm in
Lovell Township it being where George Green recently died. The same fall
of 1839, father helped James McLaughlin build his house in Castle Grove
Township..."*

Another piece of research by William E. Corbin states (30) *"To aid
the construction crews and eliminate errors on the correct location of
the surveyed route, Tilghman hired Lyman Dillon, of Cascade, to plow a*

*furrow between Iowa City and Dubuque following his line of survey mark-*
*ers. The furrow had to be done immediately during the month of August.*
*Dillon hired three men from Richland Township in Jones County. Joshua*
*and Charles Johnson would alternate with the plowing and driving the*
*covered supply wagon. John O'Sullivan would be the teamster to handle*
*and care for the ten oxen which would pull the heavy breaking plow. For*
*reasons unknown, the plowing started at Iowa City and extended 86 miles*
*to Dubuque. How long it took to plow the furrow is unknown. The oxen*
*rested at noon and turned out to graze at night. The wagon carried their*
*supplies, repair tools, cooking utensils and their blankets. The men most*
*likely slept under the wagon at night.....*

*The Langworthy brothers sublet the 25 miles of road construction*
*between Dubuque and Cascade which included most of the timbered area.*
*James Langworthy then went to work with a large crew of men and teams*
*to complete the work on road building on the open prairie between Cas-*
*cade and the Cedar River. The only bridges built were at Prairie Creek*
*and Whitewater Creek in Dubuque County and the Wapsipinicon River in*
*Jones County. All other rivers and streams had to be forded."*

*Lyman Dillon*

# 6

# Cascade To Dubuque

### September 13, 2008

I wake up refreshed. I'd spent the night in a mobile home graciously offered to me by Mr. and Mrs. James Schuester.

Larry Pisarik had (again) helped me line up some hospitality for another night of my trek. He'd approached a family he knew of whom he'd taught several of their children while they were in school. Their farm was just half of a mile or less off the Old Military Road route I was on. As I originally planned my walk, I wanted to find a place half way between Monticello and Dubuque. The James Schuester farm was the perfect location. I'd turned left off of Highway 151 at the Fillmore Catholic Church. I believe it is called Sundown Road currently. The mobile home had all the luxuries of a home. They said it was a hangout for their kids and their friends when they were back in the area. Stocked with all sorts of treats to eat, hot running water, toilet, the works.

*My hosts for the last night of my walk,*
*Mr. and Mrs. James Schuester*

When I went to bed that last night of my walk, the forecast called for heavy lightening and rain.

As I went to sleep that night I debated on whether to finish the walk - storm or no storm. Common sense won out in the end, but for a time I was strongly entertaining finishing the walk, regardless of the weather. One of the things that had gripped me as I had immersed myself in history was how hearty those people were and just how much adversity they had to deal with. Here was I, seeking to honor the memories of all these fine people, yet too soft to persevere the last day because of a little rain… Fortunately, my mettle did not have to be tested in that way. When I wake up this last morning of the walk, there is a light drizzle coming down.

There are two names in my mind as I headed down the road that last day.. Tim Fanning and his famous "log tavern" of which I had read about, and the Langworthy brothers. The tavern was the starting (or finishing) point of the Old Military Road. Today a bar, *Lot One*, sits on the spot. Another bronze historical marker is located there.

All I knew about the Langworthy family as I head into Dubuque that morning, is that there was a town named after their last name and the Langworthys had played a part in contracting a portion of Old Military Road. Researching them more would have to wait until after the walk.

I've made reservations for the evening at *Lot One* (sight of Tim Fanning's Log Tavern) for an end of walk celebration. My route takes me past another historical marker near Key West, outside of Dubuque.
Joy Adams, Micaela and I stopped to take a picture of that marker.

I have a couple of other highlights of that last day of walking. A farmer

*Local photographer took
some pictures of me as I
passed his place on my walk*

stops by in a pickup truck when he spots me. He's read about the walk in the *Dubuque Telegraph Herald* and offers me a can of pop.

The second serendipitous encounter is with a local photographer. He comes out of his house as I pass by. He wants to take a few pictures of me. Later, he sends me a large copy of a couple of them.

# The Langworthy family of Dubuque

I (Douglas) grew up just two miles west of the town of Langworthy, Iowa, but never heard anything about the Langworthy family until doing research for this book. The same could be said for every other story and person I have included in this book. We never covered any of this in school.

My life and appreciation for living right here in Eastern Iowa, in the Monticello, Anamosa, Scotch Grove, Langworthy area has grown a hundred fold since studying its local history.

I decided to tell the story of the Langworthy brothers beginning with their father, Stephen Langworthy MD. All of this information came from either the 1880 History of Dubuque County Iowa book, the Roots web genealogy website or the online *Encyclopedia Dubuque.*

Stephen served as a physician and surgeon in the U.S. Army. He was born Oct 4, 1777 in Windsor, Vermont.... died July 27, 1848 in Dubuque, Iowa.

He married Betsey Massey, who was born February 20, 1781 and died of malaria at the age of 39, leaving behind 12 children. Betsey died September 16, 1820 while the family lived in Edwardsville, Illinois.

Here is a list of their 12 children. The names in bold print I expand upon later.

**James Lyon Langworthy**:
Born January 20, 1800 in Windsor, Vermont.
Married Agnes Milnes March 17, 1840, Galena, Jo Daviess Co., Illinois.
They had five children: James, Douglas, Mary, Herbert who died at age 3, and Clara. James Langworthy died March 14, 1865, in Monticello, Iowa at the train station.

Stephen Langworthy
Born July 25, 1801, Windsor, Vermont. Died April 5, 1820 of malaria (like his mother) in Edwardsville, Illinois, age 19.

Eliza Langworthy
Born September 1803

Laura Langworthy
Born April 1, 1805, Hopkinton, St. Lawrence Co., New York. Died January 7, 1848 at 42. She was married twice. First to Jacob D. Williams who died of cholera in 1833. She married John Overstreet in 1836.

**Lucius Hart Langworthy**
Born Feb 6, 1807, Hopkinton, St. Lawrence Co., New York.
Married Mary Frances Reeder Mar 26, 1835 (he was 28). They had two children, Lucien and Oscar. Son Lucien, died when he was nine. Lucius died June 9, 1865, Dubuque, Iowa (he was 58).

**Edward Langworthy**
He was Born August 31, 1808, Rutland, New York. Married Paulina Reeder August 3, 1835, Dubuque Co., Iowa (he was 28) Died Jan 4, 1893, Dubuque, Iowa (at the ripe old age of 84). His wife had died the year previous. They had four children. Mary, Reeder, Frances and Pauline. Mary died when she was three.

Mary Ann Langworthy
Born Dec 17, 1809, Hopkinton, St. Lawrence Co., New York. She married Orrin Smith, mining partner of brother, James, in 1827 (she would have been 18 at the time). She died June 12, 1881, age 71.

Sara Maria Langworthy
Born Dec 17, 1809, Hopkinton, St. Lawrence Co., New York.
Married Captain Daniel Smith Harris May 22, 1833, Galena, Illinois. Died July 25, 1850, Havana, Cuba (age 40).

Lucretia C. Langworthy
Born September 3, 1812, Hopkinton, St. Lawrence Co., New York.
Married Gary White March 27, 1831, (she was 18). Married a second time to Purdy Williamson. Lucretia died September 18, 1854. She was 42.

**Solon Massey Langworthy**
Born January 27, 1814, Rutland, New York. He married Julia Lois Patter-

son April 20, 1840. They had eight children: Forrest, Francis Forrest, Julia Solonia, Forrest Woodbury, Lois Anna, who died when she was six, Mary, Massey and Solon Massey.

Solon Massey (the father), died June 7, 1886, age 72.

Lucien Langworthy
Born September 4, 1815. Died March 13, 1831 (age 15).

Harriet Lyon Langworthy
Born April 24, 1817. Married James Madison Marsh, December 17, 1845. She died June 13, 1854 (age 37).

At the close of the war of 1812, Stephen and his family resided in western New York, however, due to disturbances along the New York and Canadian border, as well as the difficulty of supporting so large a family, the Langworthys relocated to French Creek in Brie, Pennsylvania in 1815.

Here, Stephen erected a sawmill which employed the two oldest sons, James and Stephen (Later on, James would help erect a sawmill on the Buffalo River north of Anamosa).

Meanwhile, Stephen continued in the medical profession.

Not long after, the family pushed farther westward. For the journey, they constructed a flat-boat and the entire family descended the French Creek, The Alleghany, into the Ohio River.

*Flat bottom boat*

While passing over Letarts Falls, most of the valuable goods stowed in the boat were destroyed, the family barely escaping. (They would have included a one, three and four year old child) in addition to the other nine children, I can't imagine the terror of that experience). With their few remaining belongings, they continued to Marietta on the Ohio (summer- fall of 1818?) Here, they found the deserted, burnt out mansion of Blennerhasset on the island bearing the same name.

The famous former owner of the mansion had joined with Aaron Burr in a scheme to establish a Southern Federacy. The plan had been frustrated by Lewis Cass, then Governor of the Northwestern Territory, and the two conspirators quickly eluded pursuit using the Ohio and Mississippi rivers, never returning to the beautiful island and ruined mansion. The Langworthys camped here until spring of 1819 and then continued another four hundred fifty miles downriver by flatboat to Shawneetown, Illinois. Stephen sold the flat-boat to purchase wagons and horses, household goods, and other provisions. The family traveled 25 days (150 mile trek - averaging 6 miles a day), through southern Illinois, and settled in Edwardsville in May 1819, which was near St Louis, population three thousand. April 5, 1820, their son, Stephen Langworthy, dies of malaria. September 16, 1820. Betsey Massey Langworthy dies of malaria..." leaving behind 11 children, the youngest just three years old. As a result, the eldest son, James, decided to travel with his uncle, Dr. Isaiah Massey (his mother's brother), to seek new settlement. The family left Edwardsville for Diamond Grove, Illinois. (About 100 miles straight north), where they built a cabin and began farming.

In 1823, at 46, Dr. Langworthy returned to St. Louis briefly, leaving his children at the farm. He met and married Miss Jane Moreing, 20, three years younger than James and the same age as Eliza, the two oldest living Langworthy children. Stephen and Jane would have an additional nine children.

## James Langworthy

Born: Windsor, Vermont
January 20, 1800
Died: March 14 or May 31, 1865
Monticello, Iowa train depot

James L. was the oldest of 12 children of Dr. Stephen Langworthy and Betsey (Massey) Langworthy.

The oldest, James, left St. Louis in 1824 and began mining in Hardscrabble (now Hazel Green), Wisconsin. Three years later two other brothers, Lucius and Edward, joined him. In 1829-1830, the Langworthys crossed the river and began illegal mining activity in Dubuque's Mines of Spain. James was one of the signers of the "Miners Compact" (June 17, 1830), probably the first set of laws drawn up by settlers in what would later become Iowa.

While the natives would not allow him to mine lead, James Langworthy was permitted in 1829 to explore the entire area between the Maquoketa and Turkey rivers.

Three years later, two other brothers, Lucius and Edward, joined him. When official, white settlement was permitted in 1833 after the Black Hawk War, the Langworthys were joined by a fourth brother, Solon,

Since James was the oldest he was considered the "head of the family," yet less is known about him than his brothers. In 1849, he built a house he called the Ridgemount, on top of the Third Street bluff (now the site of Mercy Medical Center). He also constructed the first schoolhouse in Dubuque and, with his brother, Lucius, was instrumental in getting Congress to appropriate funds to construct a "military road" from Dubuque to Iowa City in 1839.

His business ventures included real estate and banking. In 1857, James's personal estate was valued at $126,090. The Langworthys owned some 600 acres of land in the city during their lifetimes. James also served in the state constitutional convention in 1844 and one term in the territorial legislature as a "free-trade Democrat."

In 1840, Mr. Langworthy married Agnes Milne, a native of Edinburgh, Scotland. Langworthy and his family made a voyage to Europe in 1846 and spent six months in visiting different parts of Great Britain and adjacent islands. Returning to Dubuque, the family lived in "the big brick house" on the corner of Iowa and 12th Street until about 1850, when he moved to the bluff at the head of Third Street.

James, Lucius, Edward and Solon entered into a co-partnership in mining, real estate, and banking which continued until all retired in 1862. So successful was the firm of *J. L. Langworthy and Bros.,* that in 1855-1856, it paid one-twelfth of the entire tax collected in Dubuque. Despite its success, the bank closed after the *Panic of 1857.*

In terms of the Old Military Road, and James Langworthy's connection with Lyman Dillon, I came across the following: (31)

*"On the 23rd of May, in that same year (1839), the engineers appointed to survey the military road from Dubuque to Iowa City, passed through the prairie, locating the road substantially where it now runs; $20,000 were at first appropriated by the General Government for surveying, bridging, grubbing and opening the same. Subsequently, $13,000 additional were appropriated for the same purpose....In the same year, 1839, James L. Langworthy of Dubuque, also took contracts for bridging, grubbing, and opening the road, paying $3 per mile for running a furrow to indicate the locality of the road. July 3, 1839, witnessed the raising of Walworth's Mill at Fisherville. Runners were sent some eighteen miles for hands to raise. Thirty were obtained. This was probably the first heavy raising in Jones County without whiskey. Strong coffee, richly prepared with sugar and cream, was used as a substitute. As the raising occupied two days, all hands encamped for the night on the ample floor. As a pastime during the evening, an interesting discussion on banking was held, George H. Walworth being in favor and James L. Langworthy opposed to the institution."*

I came across the following account of James L Langworthy's death in two sources: The 1883 History of Johnson County: (32):

*"Mr. Langworthy lived to see the naked prairie on which he first landed become the site of a city of fifteen thousand inhabitants, the small school house which he aided in constructing replaced by three substantial edifices, wherein two thousand children were being trained, churches erected in every part of the city, and railroads connecting the wilderness which he first explored with all the eastern world. He died suddenly on the 13th of March, 1865, while on a trip over the Dubuque & Southwestern Railroad at Monticello, and the evening train brought news of his death and his remains."*

In the 1910 History of Jones County, Volume 1, Martha Gallagher (33) expanded upon the circumstances of his death:

*"I don't remember anything special that happened until the surveyors came to survey for the D&SRR from Dubuque to Anamosa. Then we began to prick up our ears for scarcely one of us had ever seen a railroad or a car. The Langworthys of Dubuque were the principle figures in getting stock for the road. James Langworthy was the main one. He induced a*

*great many people to take stock in the road, and made them believe they would be getting dividends as soon as the road got to running. He got them to mortgage a piece of land to secure the purchase price of the stock subscribed for, and afterward the company sold out to another road. After some time the mortgages were foreclosed, and if the land did not bring what the mortgages called for, the parties who were worth it, had to pay the deficiency. No one ever realized a cent from the stock.*

*James Langworthy came out to collect for some of the stock, and while he was having some excitement about it on the depot platform, he suddenly fell dead. I don't think the stockholders grieved very much, for they all felt bitter towards him...." he would have been 65 years old..."*

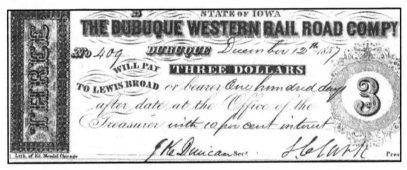

*Here is a picture of the Railroad bonds issued in 1857*
*for the Dubuque Western Railroad*

The railroad used the Dubuque and Pacific track to Farley Junction, then went its own way through Worthington, Sandsprings, and Monticello. It had reached Langworthy in 1859. The railroad went bankrupt and the bond was worth only a few cents. (34)

## Lucius Hart Langworthy

Born Hopkinton, New York,
February 6, 1807
Died: June 9 (or 30th)
Dubuque, Iowa 1865

Lucius H. Langworthy was a gifted man with ma͟

the second of twelve children by Dr. Stephen and Betsey (Massey) Lang-worthy. He was not afraid of hard physical labor. He was a miner, a soldier, the first sheriff, husband, businessman, farmer, historian, teacher, writer, banker, railroad president, co-owner of a steamboat, part owner in a news-paper for a time. He attended school at an academy in Illinois and then taught school for two years. In 1827, age 20, he joined his brother James Langworthy as a lead miner in Galena.

In 1829, James and Lucius attempted to gain control of the lead mines across the river in Dubuque. Following the unsuccessful attempt of James to get the Meskwakies to let him work the mines in 1830, they took a party of miners with them across the Mississippi River to the Dubuque mines which were then called the "New Mines." Since the land in present-day Iowa was still considered property of the Native Americans, federal troops evicted the miners twice. In 1834, he built the first frame house in Dubuque, where he also developed a large orchard. He was elected as the first sheriff of the county and was co-owner of a steamboat named *The Heroine.*

Along with others, Lucius worked diligently to develop a Pacific railroad. In 1855 (age 48), he was a director of the Dubuque & Sioux City Railroad, and subsequently became president of the Dubuque Western Railroad. He was one of the delegates who traveled to Washington, D. C. to obtain a grant for the Pacific Railroad, a line in which he was an origi-nal incorporator. He also served as one of the first directors of the Miners' Bank. He was a writer....around 1860, Lucius wrote *Sketches of the Early Settlement of the West,* one of the first histories of Dubuque. He was an amateur historian who compiled many articles and delivered lectures on literary and historical topics.

As I (Douglas), learned about Lucius, I felt a genuine connection. We were both born on February 6th. I love local history, also have an orchard, and love to teach and enjoy writing. Can't say I was ever on a bank board or owned a steamboat however...

# Edward Langworthy

Born: St. Lawrence, New York
August 3, 1808
Died: January 5, 1893
Dubuque, Iowa

Edward was, at the time of his death, the wealthiest of the four Langworthy brothers in terms of personal assets ($170,000). In today's dollars, as of 2015, that would equal $183,000,000. Like Lucius, he served in the Black Hawk War. Politically, he was the most active of the four brothers, serving in the territorial legislature for three terms, in the 1844 constitutional convention, and as a member of the trustees of the town and later as a city alderman. In 1836, he attended a railroad convention in Madison, Wisconsin, and was an early advocate for constructing a railway from Lake Michigan to the Mississippi River. He constructed his first house in 1837, the same year Dubuque was chartered as a town.

By 1854, Edward, along with his brothers James, Lucius and Solon, owned one-twelfth of all the real estate in Dubuque. They did a large banking business in Dubuque in 1855 under the name of J.L. Langworthy and Bros.

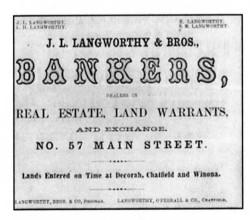

In 1856-1857, Edward and his wife Pauline hired John Francis Rague, a famous architect of the day, to design the Octagon House for them. Their house cost $8,000 to build, which in today's dollars (as of 2015) works out to just under $3,000,000.

Then, in 1857, the bottom dropped out of the economy… It was called *"The Panic of 1857."*

It was a world-wide economic crisis. Nations were now interconnected financially and the decision made in Britain set in motion a chain of events reaching as far as Dubuque, Iowa. Basically, the banks in Britain figured out a way to get around the law requiring they link the value of their money directly to the amount of gold in their possession.

(Boy, doesn't that sound familiar? Just like the banking system in the United States today, since present day banks are no longer linked to tangible assets like gold and silver).

"The tipping point that really set *The Panic of 1857* in motion was the failure of Ohio Life Insurance & Trust Company on August 24, 1857. Ohio Life was an Ohio-based bank with a second main office in New York City. The company had large mortgage holdings and was the liaison to other Ohio investment banks. Ohio Life failed due to fraudulent activities by the company's management and its failure threatened to precipitate the failure of other Ohio banks or even worse, to create a run on the banks." (35)

In 1864, Edward became a stockholder and director in the First National Bank–the first nationally chartered bank in Dubuque.

In researching this book, attempting to sort out fact from fiction, one of the most important pieces of information surrounding the details of what Lyman Dillon did and did not do, I came across the following letter written by Edward Langworthy himself dated 1882- 43 years after the furrow had been plowed. Edward himself, along with his brother James and Lucius, were the ones who had the contract to build portions of the road. The letter can be found in *The History of Johnson County 1883*. (36) I've highlighted a few details that jumped out to me. DM

Dubuque, Iowa, Aug 3, 1882

*H.A. Reid, Esq., Dear Sir:*
*In replying to yours of July 31, I have taken a part of my seventy-fourth birthday for that purpose, as it calls to my mind the very many pleasant days I have spent in your beautiful Iowa City and the many acts of kindness I have received from the citizens of that place. In its darkest days it was in my power to render your town some service in hastening the construction of the capital when almost a majority of the territorial legislature were determined on stopping its progress; and I received a very cordial invitation to partake of a public dinner there- which my duties compelled me to decline. But I told them I would spend an evening with them on my return trip home- and a happy evening it was for me, as the whole city met me with kindly greeting and very complimentary addresses. I also had the*

*pleasure of a residence, or stay, in your city, as a member of the first constitutional convention; but we made the state too large (northerly) to suit our southern friends, and it failed before the people. But my stay there was made very pleasant by my old-time friends.*

*Regarding the military road from Dubuque to Iowa City, I can give you some information. My brothers, James L. and Lucius H. and myself, had the contract to make the road from Dubuque to the Cedar River, and at the risk of taking something from the romance of the late publications, I will give the facts according to my present recollection of them. There was an appropriation for that object and it was placed in charge of a Mr. Tighlman, a U.S. Engineer, who made a thorough survey of the whole route and let the contracts, after which he directed Mr. Lyman Dillon, of Cascade, to plow a furrow on one side of the whole length of the road, which he did under the personal superintendence of the engineer, as a guide to the contractors.*

*The road was sub-let by us in small sections from here to Cascade, and the balance was done by my oldest brother, James, who had a large force of men and teams all the season at work on the road, and completed the same to the entire satisfaction of the engineer. I remember driving my carriage with some eastern friends on that road to Iowa City while the work was progressing, and after looking over the city and its surroundings we returned one afternoon and camped with my brother James and his men on the east end of the renown Linn Grove, and reached Dubuque the next day by early moonlight. In those early days, the counties of Johnson and Linn were intimately connected with Dubuque in all their business relations. It was here they sold their pork and produce, and here they found moneyed men to enter their land for them at twenty per cent interest, and here they found their political friends who joined with the people of Lee and the other southern counties, located the capital in Iowa City as against the united voice of Burlington, Fairfield and the balance of then Central Iowa and when removed it west- not south.*

*I am, dear sir, yours,*
Edward Langworthy

# Solon M. Langworthy

Born: Rutland, New York
January 17, 1814
Died: June 7, 1866
Dubuque, Iowa

Solon was tenth in line of the twelve children of Dr. Stephen and Betsey Langworthy.

To put Solon's life story in context with the rest of the family history, I will pick it up in the year 1824. Solon's oldest brother, James, set out for the Upper Mississippi lead mine area where the mineral had recently been discovered in large quantities.

Within ten days, James landed at Fever River (present-day Galena), and teamed up with Cincinnati native, Orrin Smith. They began mining at Hardscrabble, one mile east of Hazel Green, Wisconsin. After nearly two years of hard labor, (1826) the two men struck big. Eager to share the news with his family, James and his partner rode together on horseback to Diamond Grove.

The men were greeted by Dr. Langworthy and his new wife, along with the children Eliza, Laura, Lucius H., Edward, Mary Ann, Sarah Maria, Lucretia, Solon, Lucien and Harriet, as well the couple's newest arrivals, Stephen C. and William.

During the visit, Orrin caught the attention of Mary Ann (she was 17), whom he later married.

Brothers Lucius and Edward were fascinated by James and Orrin's success, and grew determined to seek the mines themselves. In the spring of 1827, Lucius (age 20), Edward (19), and Solon (13), left home with their twin sisters, Mary Ann and Maria. Traveling by wagon, they reached "Wood's Woodyard" (modern-day Quincy).

Here Solon bid farewell to his brothers and sisters as they boarded a steamboat headed for James and Orrin's mining town... which was 250 miles upriver on the Mississippi.

Solon returned to Diamond Grove, now the eldest brother still residing there (age 13). With the assistance of his younger brother, Lucien and another man, he managed the farm consisting of more than one hundred acres.

Farming with horse or ox…can't imagine farming that much ground in those days.

Soon after her arrival in the lead mining country, Mary Ann (age 18), fulfilled her promise to marry Orrin Smith, Maria (Sara Maria, her twin sister), sharing their home. Maria would later marry Captain Daniel Smith Harris in 1833.

The marriage was followed by those of Eliza, (age 24) marrying William Maclay, and Laura, (age 22) marrying Jacob D. Williams, both in 1827. (At this time in Wisconsin's early history and development, women were rare which explains [to me] the speed at which all three young ladies found husbands).

Meanwhile, Lucius (21) and Edward (20), settled in a cabin in Coon Branch, also near Hazel Green and began mining.

In April 1828, Solon (age 14), left Diamond Grove with Horace McCartney and headed for Galena, Illinois.

Inhabitants were scarce between the two towns. Although natives had sold these lands, many still remained, slowing white settlement. Solon and Horace had traveled a short distance west of the Illinois River when they met a party of drovers en route for the mines. They were strongly advised not to journey alone, and joined the drovers for six or seven days. Once they were within 20 miles of Rock River, their provisions nearly exhausted, they left the slow-traveling drovers to press on more quickly. As they approached the river, however, a large body of mounted Indians surrounded them.

Two chiefs, communicating through gestures and broken mutterings, inquired as to the business and destination of the two travelers and examined their equipment. Next, they signaled the voyagers to follow them. In minutes, the entire party was on the banks of the Rock River. Solon and Horace asked the chiefs for the use of their canoes to cross the river, but were denied. Young natives sportively wrestled with the travelers before the men continued across the river by horse.

When they reached Council Hill, the men separated and Solon set out for Buncomb to meet his brother James. The following day, Solon and James continued to the mining cabin on Coon Branch where Lucius and Edward lived. For the first time in several years, the four brothers were reunited. 1828-1831

Orrin Smith joined the brothers and invited Solon to his residence on the Platte (British Hollow). Here, he visited his two sisters before returning to Coon Branch, where he resided that summer with Lucius and Edward. As a miner, the season proved fortunate, enabling Solon to revisit Diamond Grove in November, 1828, accompanied by James Meredith.

The next three years were devoted to labor upon the farm, which sold in 1831, the remaining family members (all siblings now totaling 21), moving to St. Charles, Missouri.

Solon now found employment with a neighboring farmer.

1832; Becoming dissatisfied with that business in July, 1832, Solon enlisted in Company A, United States Ranging Service, commanded by Captain Nathaniel Boone, grandson of the famous Daniel Boone. He reported to General Winfield Scott at Rock Island, August 20, 1832, whereafter the company encamped below the garrison. In the weeks following, cholera made its appearance in the garrison, creating great alarm. (cholera and malaria were big killers in those days).

Cholera resulted in rapid dehydration due to vomiting and diarrhea. It is a bacteria that settles in the lower intestine; unsanitary conditions were a big factor in its spreading. If acted upon, a simple oral rehydration technique, plus sanitary conditions could stop the spread. (Oral rehydration was pushing fluids mixed with a little sugar and salt and continuing to eat).

The company obtained permission to make a fresh camp south of the Rock River, just six miles away. Twelve of its members died of the malady, a slight mortality compared with that of the garrison.

August 1st and 2nd, 1832, *Battle of Bad Ax*. This battle marked the end of the Black Hawk War between the militia, and the Sauk and Fox tribes under Black Hawk. (James Langworthy would have been present).

1833 Solon, along with Ezra Overall, and William H. and Jesse Moureing, returned to their Missouri homes discharged from military service.

Upon reaching St. Charles, Solon discovered that his brother-in-law, Mr. Williams, had died of cholera. He remained with his sister, Laura, during the winter to help her settle the estate.

In the spring of 1834, Solon left for St. Louis on the steamer, Olive Branch, headed for Galena. Here he met his sister, Maria, who had become the wife of Captain Smith Harris. Traveling on the captain's boat, the Jo Daviess, Solon visited Dubuque the following day. Here he became the guest of his three brothers in their mining cabin in Langworthy Hollow.

He started working for his brothers hauling rails for fencing a farm at the heart of the city. In June, Solon became the first to plow land in Iowa, breaking up sixty acres. When the farm work was finished, he was ready to begin his career in mining.

In the fall of 1834, he purchased a large mineral lot on the Maquoketa. His brother, Lucius (age twenty-seven), worked alongside of him and together they struck a decent prospect after just two weeks. They built a cabin on the site, and Lucius returned to Dubuque while Solon lived in the cabin. He hired two men and continued mining there for a year-and-a-half. In the autumn of 1835, he bought a second potential mining spot on the Ewing Range. After blasting for about a month, he discovered a large cave filled with shining ore, inspiring him toward further mining endeavors.

In the spring of 1836, Solon entered into a partnership with Orrin Smith his brother in law. Together they mined places on Fever River (also known as the Galena River) and Coon Branch, purchasing a claim of 2,000 pounds on Coon Branch for $800.00, and exhausting it in one day. After deserting the spot, Orrin Smith left for Cincinnati while Solon met four Jemison brothers from Missouri just days later, buying their lot, cabin, tools, and lead, which was already on the surface. Paying just $2,500.00, (which doesn't seem like a lot but in today's money that would work out to between 1.3 and 28.4 MILLION dollars), he acquired between 60 and 70,000 pounds of mineral already extracted. After two months of further excavation, he was able to sell over three hundred and 50,000 pounds of mineral.

He had hired four men to assist in the operation, but after all expenses still profited $4,000.00 (2.2 to 45 MILLION dollars) which he split with his partner, Orrin Smith.

Winter of 1837; By the end of the year, profits had increased to about $22,000.00, a large portion of which was invested in the steamer, *Brazil*, built by Orrin Smith in Cincinnati in the winter of 1837. The vessel was the first ever to embark upon the Upper Mississippi. After making a few very successful trips between Cincinnati and Dubuque, the steamer wrecked on the upper rapids of the Mississippi and sunk, entirely uninsured. (This would have been a trip of more than 900 miles by river).

The following autumn, Solon started a new business venture with Henry L. Massey. (They saw an opportunity to sell work clothes to the miners... just like Levi Straus did in the California Gold Rush). Solon went to St. Louis via horseback, navigation being closed, and purchased four horses, a wagon, and a stock of clothing valued at $4,000.00. While Solon left for Cincinnati to seek stockholding options, Massey took charge of the team and headed through the state of Missouri and the Territory of Iowa to Snake Diggings, now Potosi, Wisconsin (20 miles north of Dubuque).

Due to the discovery of large quantities of mineral, a great number of miners were settled in the area, to whom Henry sold the goods. Henry sent the money to Solon in Cincinnati, who invested the profit in new stock. (of clothing). Mr. Massey continued carrying on business at Potosi until the fall of 1838, when Solon returned to run the business himself.

On April 20, 1840, Solon (age 26), married Julia L. Patterson (17), daughter of Myron and Frances Patterson of Long Island. The couple resided in Potosi until 1848. In 1848, Solon, Julia, and their six children, moved to Dubuque. 1854 - (age 40), Solon joins his brothers James, Edward and Lucius in business. In 1856, he built his imposing Greek Revival-style home. This was the same year Edmund was building his octagon house, and right before the economic crash of 1857. In 1861, during the Civil War, he supplied many fruits and vegetables to Union soldiers stationed at Camp Union (Franklin) north of Dubuque.

1862 - Solon Langworthy (age 48), was appointed Lieutenant and Quartermaster of the 27th I.V. Later in 1862, Solon was taken prisoner at Holly Springs but was later exchanged for Confederate prisoners. He returns home in 1864. Thereafter, he engaged in various enterprises, including banking, lumbering, and similar occupations. Solon and Julia's family was composed of three daughters and three sons: Solon Massey Langworthy (wife Ora), Mary (Langworthy) Bunting, Julia Solonia (Langworthy), Stephens, Frances L. (Langworthy) Poole, and Forrest W. Langworthy.

In 1886, Solon died (age 72), leaving his estate to Julia and his children.

In 1907, Julia died (21 years after Solon), leaving the estate to her children, Mary, Solonia, Frances, Forrest and Solon Massey.


# Tim Fanning

Born in Ireland, 1810

Died: February 17, 1863

He lived to be 53 years old


*"Tim was a tall, lanky, good natured Irishman. His was the only hotel in town. Being a double log cabin, that is, twice the usual length and two stories high, it had sufficient accommodations for the traveler of that day."*
*— Edmund Booth*


There is not the wealth of information on Tim Fanning to be found compared to the Langworthy brothers. Following are a few stories and bits and pieces of information.

Tim Fanning was married to Elizabeth P. Fanning. (37) As of this writing, I was not able to find her maiden name. They had three children, losing them all at an early age. Lucy Fanning…1841-1842, died when she was one. Valentine Fanning, died at three months of age in 1846, and Michael Fanning…died at age six in 1847. Lots of heartache. Having babies and raising a young family on the edge of the western frontier was not for the faint of heart.

Timothy Fanning came to Dubuque in 1836. Tim definitely had a business head on his shoulders. In addition to running the Log Tavern and hotel known as the "Jefferson House," he also operated the main ferry business across the Mississippi between Dubuque and East Dubuque. It was a great combination. After you crossed the mighty Mississippi and you needed lodging or a drink, there was Tim's hotel, right near the dock.

In December, 1838, an act of the Iowa territorial legislature authorized Timothy Fanning to operate a ferry at Dubuque for twenty years. He was required to land at any required part of the river front of the town to keep ample boats and facilities and two years later, was to put on a steam ferryboat and a sufficient number of flatboats.

By 1840, Fanning had a steam powered ferry. In 1855, he added another large steam ferry, The Queen City, to serve the Wisconsin shore area.

Edmund Booth (whom I wrote about earlier in my chapter on Anamosa), mentioned Tim Fanning and the Log Tavern in his recollections of his first trip to Iowa:

*"I arrived at 'the Forks,' as they were familiarly termed—meaning Buffalo Forks of the Wapsipinicon, often abbreviated to Wapsi—in August, 1839. If I remember aright, it was on the 18th of August. I had reached Dubuque from the east some days previously…*

*In the course of the evening, after seeing Mr. Davis as above described, he called on me at Tim Fanning's, Log Tavern, the only hotel in Dubuque, and informed me that two men would start next morning for Iowa City, then just laid out as the capital of the Territory of Iowa. They were going to attend the first sale of lots…."*  – Edmund Booth

Tim Fanning is mentioned briefly in an incident that happened in 1840. (38) There are two Fanning men mentioned in the account. I'm guessing they were related, but at this point, it is only a guess.

*"In June 1840, a man named Storey, was shot dead by James Fanning*

*on the bank of the slough south of Third Street under the following circum-
stances. A married man named John Patterson, had employed his wife's
sister who resided with the family to assist about the house. While living in
this relation, Patterson sought to impress the girl with faith in the doctrine
taught at Nauvoo about that time by Joseph Smith. (Mormonism/ multiple
wives). The girl refused to be convinced or listen to his arguments and
demurred to his plea with a vehemence born of her womanly abhorrence
for the doctrine of polygamy which only inspired her brother in law to
renewed efforts.*

*Disgusted and alarmed at his pertinacity, she fled from the household
and sought protection at the hands of Timothy Fanning, who then kept the
Jefferson House on Main Street between First Street and the slough.*

*About 5 o'clock on the afternoon of the tragedy the man, Storey, at the
instigation of Patterson, procured a skiff and placing it in a convenient
locality near Fanning's suddenly appeared at the house and securing the
object of his visit attempted to gain the skiff before the crowd which had
been attracted by his maneuvers could overhaul and detain him. (In other
words, Storey attempted to kidnap the woman and haul her across the
Mississippi). In this, he was prevented however for James Fanning cut off
his retreat and brought the fugitive to bay before the landing place had
been attained. Storey dropped his burden and drawing a pistol fired at
Fanning wounding him in the foot as the crowd who joined in the chase
came up. There being an appearance of sympathy for Fanning, Storey
asked for fair play remarking at the same time he had no friends. Gen
Francis Gehon who was present assured him he should be protected and
William Smith (the same person Louisa Massey encountered in Guerin's
saloon four years previous), handed Fanning a brace of pistol. The fu-
sillade was renewed and at the third shot Storey fell with his head to the
north where he lay and after a convulsive gasp stiffened with death. The
body was buried at once and Fanning after undergoing the formality of a
trial was acquitted."*

So popular was the hospitality of the tavern that the state's first St.
Patrick's Day celebration was held there. (39)

*"The first celebration of St. Patrick's Day in the State of Iowa was held
in the city of Dubuque on March 17, 1838...sixty gentlemen sat down to a
festive dinner...at the Fanning Hotel...Thirteen toasts were raised to the
occasion."*

According to an early edition of *The Missouri Times*, people came from far and near to invoke the "higher powers" of the "Wishing Willow" in Fanning's Log Tavern. Fanning felled a huge tree to provide docking room for his ferry boat, which ran across Dubuque and East Dubuque.

Fanning had cut down a large willow tree and dropped it into the river to dock his boat. At some point, he took the gnarled stump into the tavern, made it into a table on which people would dance and make a wish.

The first meeting to consider organizing a Masonic Lodge in Dubuque was held on July 18, 1842. Those in attendance included Timothy Fanning. On October 10, 1842, the request for the first Masonic Lodge in Dubuque was granted by the Grand Lodge of Missouri. Timothy Fanning was named the first *Worshipful Master*.

Fanning was also involved in local politics in Dubuque. He served as an alderman in 1841, 1843, 1844 and 1845.

In April, 1852, Timothy Fanning's construction here of a steam ferryboat caused the newspapers to observe that there was no reason why Dubuque should not become a boat-building center. In 1853, he was involved in Fanning vs. Gregoire and Bogg, one of the earliest important legal cases in the history of Iowa, which eventually went all the way to the United States Supreme Court.

Back to the present (2008)

It is hard to put into words what I am feeling as I cross Catfish Creek and head up Whiskey Hill. I wish I could spend more time soaking up the multiple stories and memories of these early settlers. In part, that was one of the intentions of this book: to keep their stories alive just a bit longer.

Finally, I arrive at my destination….the very spot on which Tim Fanning's Log Tavern used to sit- *Lot One*. We take a few pictures of the moment and come back later for some merriment. I had reserved a room upstairs to celebrate the event. A handful of friends, family, and even a few local people from Dubuque join us.

No dancing on the magic willow stump to make a wish….but a quiet sense of accomplishment and thankfulness fill my heart.

*Bronze plaque marking Tim Fanning's Log Tavern*

*Just as I crossed the finish line at the corner of first and main Dubuque, Iowa 2008*

*Day I found Lyman Dillon's tombstone in Cascade*

# 7

# Gus Norlin's Research

## Lyman Dillon and His Furrow

## Original Research by Gus Norlin

W
hile the writer makes no pretext at being anything other than an amateur researcher (and certainly doesn't profess to be a writer) he does insist that when something comes along that strikes his fancy and needs digging into, he grabs: hold like a gila monster on a desert fox's foot and doesn't let up until there's no fight or challenge left.

Such has been the case with researching "Dillon's Furrow." I will make claims to this story that are in conflict somewhat with earlier researchers, and these predecessors in the research have more reason to oppose one another than they do me. These earlier researchers were either from Dubuque or Iowa City. For better than 120 years (or since Dillon died) they have argued about whether he plowed the furrow from Iowa City to Dubuque or the other way around. I have my own ideas based upon my research and first hand communication with one of the last surviving descendent of Dillon – his grand-daughter, now 98 years of age. Her information came from her mother, Dillon's daughter, Lena. More on the family later.

So that you the reader might know where my research differs from others who have written of the furrow, I will underline those statements. I have received much help and information from many and varied sources over the past 15 years of the search. Probably the most intimate and pertinent as come from Florence Lippert of Oceanside, California. She is the granddaughter I mentioned earlier. Ohers include Patrick Lean of Oxford, Iowa. Bernice Dvorsky of Iowa City. Mrs. L.C. Rohret, of Columbus Junction, Iowa. Irving B. Weber, of Iowa City, Mrs. Joe Zollar, of Cascade, and a host of others. During 1981, I sought help in making some determinations by writing a short piece in a national publication. I had good response, the most helpful coming from Roy I. Borden, of Liberal,

Kansas. While not a relative of Dillons, Mr. Borden was well acquainted with the problems that had faced Dillon. Mr. Borden, beginning at the age of 12, had plowed sod having graduated to "4 up." He told me he could see no reason for Dillon having need for any more than "4 up" or two yoke of oxen. He maintained the two yoke of oxen would be in finer flesh at the end of the journey than when they started. My research indicates he used two yoke (four oxen) as opposed to some earlier research that mentions five yoke or ten animals. Mr. Borden goes on to say he believes the sod buster would have been a sixteen inch, set to cut a four inch depth. He points out further that the distance was approximately one hundred miles or the equivalent of Dillon plowing 15.8 acres of sod. From his personal family album of pictures he had reproduced for me a photo showing his father in law plowing virgin prairie sod with what he believes would have been an identical set up to what Dillon used. The photo accompanies this article.

There was recorded on October 19, 1939, in book 169 page 219, a sworn statement by Mr. George W. Parrott of Cascade, Iowa, the son-in-law of Lyman Dillon, attesting to the fact that he had engaged in many conversations with his father-in-law, Mr. Dillon, pertaining to the facts surrounding the plowing of the furrow. These conversations, according to the statement, covered a span of many years. I believe Mr. Parrott to have been mistaken in some parts of the statement for he was 87 years of age at the time of the statement and only five years of age when Mr. Dillon died in 1857. It is possible I have overlooked something here.

Much has been written about Lyman Dillon. Most of it fact – much of it fiction. He has been typed by many as a rough and tough, two fisted, hard drinking, square jawed sod bustin, bootlegging mill-man. He was not! In fact, he was quite the opposite. He has also been referred to as "generous to a fault," compassionate, extremely soft hearted, a wonderful family man, more benevolent that most early pioneers. This he was. He partook of the "swig of corn" sparingly. His greatest vice was probably "chawin tobacco." It killed him. He died of cancer of the jaw on December 8, 1857. He was 57 years of age.

Lyman Dillon, who is generally remembered only as the man who plowed a furrow between Dubuque and Iowa City. You will note, I did not say from Dubuque to Iowa City, although my research is closing the gap on "from where to where" was born at Utica, New York on June 12, 1800. He had one younger brother, and the two boys were orphaned when still very young. Both boys were "bound out" (not adopted) the young one to a minister and Lyman to a tavern keeper. The younger brother became a minister but fell ill and died shortly after "beginning his preachin." Lyman found the task extremely hard for he had been bound to a regular slave driving man, and even at the tender age was expected to unload drays stacked with barreled beer. These had to be rolled into the storage rooms and stacked on end. Then there was the constant keeping the tavern clean, and the washing of mugs. It seemed that everyone did nothing but drink beer, and there must have been a million mugs a day to wash and rinse. Dillon soon resolved to get away from this one way or another, for he had a burning desire to become educated, even though there was little opportunity at that time and place. Books were almost unheard of and newspapers scarce, but with encouragement from travelers stopping at the tavern, he finally ran away, gaining some primary education and eventually enrolling at a college in Utica. He worked for his board and room and earned enough to pay tuition. He graduated from college, then followed Greeley's well known admonition and "went west." He was still a young man when after having saved a little money, he bought a tract of land from the Government. The tract was located near Cascade.

Now I should make a clarification when say he was "still a young man" for he was approaching 37 years of age. Quite frankly, in those days, a man of 37 was looked upon as having gone well past middle age. Mortality tables show that men could be expected to reach 54 years of age back in 1840. Of course many exceeded that – many more did not reach it.

Dillon now had a tract of ground but no implements to break the sod or till the ground to which he wished to plant wheat. It was necessary that he find work and earn enough to purchase the basic tools for farming. He was noted as "one of the best bull whackers" or ox drivers in these parts, and he had come to Cascade with two yokes (four ox) of these fine animals, having made the journey with them from Ohio. In order to earn extra money, he took his teams to Dubuque and entered into the "dray" business. During the course of his self-employment as a drayman, he became acquainted with the Langworthy brothers, undoubtedly through doing business with them… (The next three lines of this paper are illegible)…used every phrase imaginable to entice the westward traveling pioneer to go to Iowa City from Dubuque where they would find utopia, whether their gain to be as farmers or merchants or one of the professions. While the advertising was all honest and above board, there was a serious drawback. Not much of a trail existed between those two points. Surely not as good as a trail as existed from Dubuque almost straight west through Independence and on to Missouri. This at least was a trail a man could have little trouble following, for enough traffic existed that the head high "Buffalo" and other prairie grasses had been ground down to the roots, leaving a path that could be followed without too much difficulty. The occasional traveler to Iowa City from Dubuque almost had to blaze a new trail each time it was traversed. It seemed the grass would spring up to immense heights almost overnight. The Langworthys knew this was deterring a great many potential land buyers away from Iowa City. Some way must be found to have them head in the direction of Iowa City, not Sioux City on the Missouri. Now there is where some of my research conflicts with research done by others...but most closely asserts itself with the research done by F. L. Baldwin in 1929.

Lucius Langworthy, a man of means, approached Dillon and inquired if he knew the shortest and best route to Iowa City, then the newly designated State Capital. Dillon replied that he had been to Iowa City, knew a route, but not necessarily the "best route" as he had never had occasion to search for the best stream crossings or routes around bogs or swamp areas. Langworthy pressed on. "Would Dillon be for hire to first make a rough trail breaking survey, and after that determination, could he be hired to plow a furrow between the two points?"

Dillon answered in the affirmative to both questions, inquiring as to the reason Langworthy wished this furrow plowed, Langworthy explained his personal reasons. Dillon determined to begin at Dubuque with his on foot "survey trek", in other words, he would walk to Iowa City then, while there, procure the necessary equipage and plow the furrow back. One thing bothered him; he must design a breaking plow (and buster) with replaceable steel shares, a tailed off landslide of one piece and a mouldboard with an acutely curled tail off that would cause the ribbon of sod to break as it fell from the mouldboard thereby assuring that the sod strip not uncurl and fall back into the newly plowed furrow. It is extremely doubtful that the plow was of anything near the 30 inch dimension as purported in some stories on the furrow. A plow cutting a furrow 30 inches wide and four inches deep would have taken two men to control. It is more likely to have been a 16 incher, which in sod busting days was immense. Twelve inches was a standard size, and even this required a good man in order to handle it.

[*Ed. note; the writer knows a little of what he is saying, having broken with just such a plow behind horses...in Iowa. This was, as a farm boy, living almost in the middle of "Snell's Slew" south of Fort Dodge, Iowa).*

In doing research for this article I interviewed many old timer who also had experience with bustin sod. None could fathom a plow cutting a 30 inch furrow, or even the need for a furrow of this width. All maintained that a 16 inch strip could be tamed to roll over and lay flat if the moldboard tail were of proper "sod busting" design. Dillon was worried he would be unable to find a "smithy" in the new territorial capital who would have either the expertise or material to fashion the type of plow he would need. He knew there was any number of qualified Smiths in Dubuque, and perhaps time could be saved if such a plow were built there. This would mean that while he was laying out the route the Smith could be building the plow, and he could return from Iowa City to Dubuque by horseback, only a two day journey. The furrow would then be plowed from Dubuque to Iowa City. Did he purchase the oxen in Iowa City? We do not know where the plow was built. His determination of the best route by a walking survey took about two weeks, and as soon as he reached the Capital City he began making preparations to return to Dubuque. He purchased the oxen from Eli Myers. No evidence exists that he purchased a team of horses and wagon for the spare parts or supplies that must have be taken along during the plowing. We do know that he hired two boys or young men, they being John and George Rohret who lived in the area called "Old man's Creek" slightly west of the then Iowa City. It was necessary that two helpers be hired, for one must tend to the wagon and supplies, and one to walk alongside the oxen while they plowed. Oxen were not controlled by lines from the plowman as were horses. Most oxen were trained to respond to the GEE and HAW commands, and when hearing the command to GEE would swing slightly to the left. HAW was the command to swing right. Animals, not as well trained, would have a heavy leather strap or light chain attached to the neck and if not responding to verbal commands, the chain would be pulled to indicate the direction they should veer to.

All preparations having been made, all supplies having been loaded, Dillon and his help began plowing the furrow. It is evident he chose a good route, for the present Highway 1 from Iowa City to Mount Vernon and that portion of Highway 151 from Springville to Dubuque still largely follows the original furrow.

A survey by the civilian engineer from Baltimore, R.C. Tilghman, some six months AFTER Dillon plowed his furrow and the trail turns south from Pamaho (now Fairview in Jones County), and follows a line to Martelle then to Mount Vernon. Mr. Tilghman had more resources at his command for he was doing this survey for the government, and the fact that much of the land between Pamaho and Mount Vernon was swamp, almost one huge lake was no deterrent. He was making a survey for the

Government and the road would be built and for the military. This swamp obstacle to Dillon meant circumventing it so he did, going west from Pamaho to the present Springville, then south and east to the present site of Mount Vernon. (Now if you believe Dillon started at Iowa City then he plowed north to Mount Vernon then west by north to Springville, then east to Pamaho). It was to his advantage to follow the ridges and timberlines, and unless the reader has ever had the opportunity to see early maps of the area which Dillon plowed his furrow, no way can the reader envision how heavily wooded portions of this part of Iowa were. As a case in point, Dillon's Furrow from Monticello (then called Varvels Place), to Cascade (then called Fountain Falls), leads north by east from Monticello for a distance of about 4 miles, then angles slightly to east by north for approximately one mile, then abruptly angles east into Cascade. It would have been shorter to angle Northeast directly from Monticello to Cascade but the timber was dense and Dillon followed the timberline between these two points.

I remember when first beginning some research on Dillon 30 some years ago, of having read and been told by the "old timers" that Dillon knew where all of the early homesteads were between Dubuque and Iowa City, and at which places he could get a good stiff drink, and because of this, he plowed such a crooked furrow. Well, we know that isn't so. After fulfilling his contract with Langworthy, Dillon returned to Cascade and then married a girl by the name of Winchell. About this same time he purchased from the Delong brothers a saw mill located on the north fork of the Maquoketa River a short distance north of Cascade.

His family of six children, the eldest a girl named Cordelia. The second child, also a girl, was Luella. The third child was a boy whom they named Alvin. The fourth child was Maria, followed by Lena. I believe the last child to have been a girl, Florence. Lyman Dillon, his wife and three of the children, Cordelia, Lena and Marie are buried in Cascade.

Very shortly after completing the furrow, when it became evident that such a trail would not suffice because of the rapidity with which the growing prairie grasses were beginning to obliterate it, pressure was brought to bear on the Federal government to improve the route. It was impossible to get funding just to improve a road for westward moving settlers, but under the guise of creating a road for the military, $20,000.00 was appropriated to improve the route from Dubuque to the Missouri border via Iowa City. First, it would be necessary to have a suitable survey made, and at this time, mounds of earth were built up so that the construction crew to come later would have markers to follow. Little thought was giving to proper grade of the road, and not much more was given to proper construction of bridges over the streams. The construction was done in large part by men of the military under command of Jefferson Davis, who later was to become president of the Confederacy. There remains today about one mile of the actual furrowed trail later improved by the military. This had been abandoned some thirty years, but pretty much remains intact by reason of a fenced road. It is located between Monticello and Langworthy approximately one mile west of the present Highway 151.

---

# Correspondence between
# Gus and Irving Weber
# pertaining to Dillon's Furrow:

IRVING B. WEBER
421 MELROSE COURT
IOWA CITY, IOWA 52240
(319) 337-7966

February 14, 1981

Mr. C. L. Norlin,
923 N. Chestnut Street,
Monticello, Iowa;

Dear Mr. Norlin:-

      I was most interested in your letter
"To The Editor" of the Iowa Cilty Press-Citizen about
Lyman Dillon and his plowing of the 100 mile furrow
from Iowa City to Dubuque in 1839; and you are right
it was from Iowa City to Dubuque and not vice versa.
I write historical articles for the Iowa City Press-
Citizen and have m.entioned Dillon's Furrow, the National
Road, the Military Road from time tto time.

      I am enclosing and article I wrote on the
town of Solon, 12 miles north of Iowa City, that was
on Dillon's Furrow. There is quite a little data on
the rod there.

              letter
      When I read your article I thought that
the man you were inquiring about was L. C. (Wink) Rohret,
a long time friend o f mine, and a great historian.
He died last summer. He was living in Columbus City
(his wife still does) AT THE TIME. I went to his funeral
at Cosgrove, 10 miles west of Iowa City.

      Rohret had told me that one of his great
uncles had helped Dillon plow the road and he seemed to
know a great deal .about .it. I called Rohret's neice, Mi
Mary Heal 322 N. Linn Street, Iowa City, Phone 337 3269,
Mary Healy
but she reminded me that Rohret was not well enough that
he would have been to see you 2 years ago. I believe
Miss Healy is going to write you. She had seen you letter
as had also Mrs. Richard (Berneice Rohret)Dvorsky (RR #2,
Iowa City). I understand she was going to send you a
letter. She and Miss Healy both helped Rohret in the
very complete Roh.ret Genealogy, with much Iowa City
history.

      The 1836-1882 History of Johnson County,
pages 235, 236 has information about the Furrow;
also Shambaugh's "The Old Stone Capitol Remembers", on
pages 76 and 115 has some information on Dillon.

      Both of these books are at the State Historica
Society, 402 E. Iowa Avenue. They also have a copy of
the Palimpsest with a story by a University Iowa

IRVING B. WEBER
421 MELROSE COURT
IOWA CITY, IOWA 52240

(319) 337-7966

History Professor who walked the 100 mile furrow and
wrote about it. His name was Briggs, and if they have
any copes left you could get one for 50¢. Or go to
the Library and read it there. They may also have
other material. I presume histories of Jones County
and Dubuque County would have information and they have
those histories there I am quite sure. They are very
helpful and accommodating and would give you assistance.

Dillon was a resident apparently at one time
of Iowa City as he is noted as owning 8 lots here in
1841, though I had always heard he was from Cascade.

Eearly maps of Iowa City show a long island
in the Iowa River called Dillon's Island. Stories go
around that the island disappeared over night. However
I don't think that is quite correct. I think it disappeared after the University put in the Burlington
Street dam of the Iowa River, 1905-06

One of my avid readers just called to be sure
I saw your letter and wrote you. I'd be interested in
hearing more of what you know about Dillon and the
Furrow.

You can see the Iowa City Press-Citizen's
"letters to the editor" are well read. It's a fine paper and
they give me great leway in writing articles on historical
matters. So far in 8 years I have written 843 articles.

Yours truly,

Irving B. Weber.

# Epilogue

For several years I have wondered what it was about local history that stirs me so? Was it just the thrill of discovery? A lust for knowledge? It wasn't until just recently that I have finally been able to articulate what feeds this inner fire; their stories give me perspective.

When I read about the suffering and obstacles the Langworthy family overcame, especially in those early years, moving hundreds of miles from home, surviving disease, war, raging rivers, it gives me perspective on how good I have it.

When I read about harsh Midwest winter storms dumping two feet of snow and ice and young families trying to keep warm in a 12 by 16 foot claim cabin and all they had to eat was corn dodgers, salted pork and coffee, it gives perspective on how comfortable I have it.

When I read about an economic bubble popping in our nation in 1837 and again in 1857 which plunged our country into years of extreme deprivation, it brings perspective in these uncertain economic times. There is something to be said about having your mortgage paid off, regardless of what the financial "experts" tell us.

And while not everyone from those early years in Iowa was a person of faith, many of them did have a "Biblical worldview", John Lovejoy in particular.

## The Overton Window, local history, and worldviews

Ever hear of something called "The Overton Window?"

I was first exposed to the concept after reading an exchange between Congressman Frank Wolf and one of my favorite authors, Andreu Seu Petersen.

Wolf asked Petersen if she'd ever heard of *The Overton Window*? "Nope." He held out his hands and framed them into a window. I'm paraphrasing the conversation as I remember it:

*"Imagine a yardstick. On either end are the extremes of any issue. Between the ends lie all gradations of thought from one extreme to the other. The essence of The Overton Window is that only a portion of the spectrum is within the realm of the popular thought at any time..."*

What once was considered unthinkable goes through several steps until it becomes policy:

- Unthinkable
- Radical
- Acceptable
- Sensible
- Popular
- Policy

The Overton Window is a great word picture for me and helps me make sense of the shifting sands of cultural values.

Reading and discovering local history gives me perspective and helps keep me grounded as the lines between right and wrong, truth and lies continue to blur. As of this writing, I have a website connected with this project: *onthetrailoflymandillon.wordpress.com/*

Additional copies of this book should be available on line at Amazon, Barnes & Noble, or contacting me directly at the above mentioned website.

Douglas Monk ©2016

# Foot notes

## Introduction

(a) History of Johnson County, Iowa, from 1836 to 1882. Iowa City, 1882. Reprinted by Higginson Book Company, 148 Washington Street, P.O. Box 778 Salem, Massachusetts 01970.
(b) History of Johnson County, Iowa, from 1836 to 1882. Iowa City;1882 Reprinted by Higginson Book Company, 148 Washington Street, P.O. Box 778 Salem, Massachusetts 01970.

### Chapter 1

(1) Edited by John C. Parish; The Palimpsest Volume ll, February, 1921 No. 2. State Historical Society of Iowa, copyright 1921.
(2) Photo of John E Briggs and Marcus L. Hansen. Used with permission from original collection of photos from the *State Historical Society of Iowa* in Iowa City.
(3) Source information on Chauncey Swan; sources include the *Journal of the House of Representatives for the First and Second Legislative Assemblies of the Territory of Iowa*, 1838 and 1839; Benjamin F. Shambaugh, Iowa City: *A Contribution to the Early History of Iowa* (1893) and Benjamin Franklin Shambaugh, *The Old Stone Capitol Remembers* (1939). "Swan, Chauncey" The Biographical Dictionary of Iowa. *University of Iowa Press*, 2009. Web. 9, January, 2015.
(4) Photos of Phillip Clark used with permission from original collection of photos from the *State Historical Society of Iowa* in Iowa City.
(5) *History of Johnson County*, Iowa, from 1836 to 1882. Iowa City; 1882 page 305. Reprinted by Higginson Book Company, 148 Washington Street, P.O. Box 778 Salem, Massachusetts 01970.
(6) Benjamin F. Shambaugh M.A. Iowa City. *A Contribution to the Early History of Iowa* published by *The State Historical Society of Iowa*, Iowa City, Iowa. 1893 page 20
(7) *History of Johnson County*, Iowa, from 1836 to 1882. Iowa City; 1882 Reprinted by Higginson Book Company, 148 Washington Street, P.O. Box 778 Salem, Massachusetts 01970
(8) *History of Johnson County*, Iowa, from 1836 to 1882. Iowa City;1882 page 216, 217. Reprinted by Higginson Book Company, 148 Washington Street, P.O. Box 778, Salem, Massachusetts 01970

## Chapter 2

(9) *History of Johnson County, Iowa*, from 1836 to 1882. Iowa City, 1882 page 572-573. Reprinted by Higginson Book Company 148 Washington Street, P.O. Box 778 Salem, Massachusetts 01970.

(10) Published by The Centennial Committee, A Centennial History of Mount Vernon, Iowa 1847-1947. Hawkeye Record Press, Mt Vernon, Iowa 1948. Page 19.

(11) Published by The Centennial Committee, *A Centennial History of Mount Vernon*, Iowa 1847-1947. Hawkeye Record Press, Mt Vernon, Iowa 1948. Page 17.

## Chapter 3

(12) *Anamosa Eureka* dated October 28, 1909.

(13) Photos of Edmund and Mary Ann Booth from www.findagrave.com (Wilma Spice).

(14) *The Jan Joaquin Pioneer and Historical Society,* San Joaquin County, California 1953.

(15) R.M. Corbit, B.S. and LL.B Editor-In-Chief, *History Of Jones County Past and Present. Chicago,* published by S.J. Clark Publishing Company 1910.

## Chapter 4

(16) *The History Of Jones County* 1879 (reprint) in 1979 for the Jones County Historical Society by The Print Shop, Dixon, Illinois 1979

(17) Iowa Sketches - John Newton Hughes edited by Michele Shover and published by Penwoman Publication in 1992.

(18) 1937 Centennial booklet on Scotch Grove.

(19) Original picture of Scottish ox cart at Bill Corbin residence, Monticello, Iowa.

(20) From *The Land Atlas And Pictorial Directory Of Jones County Iowa.* Compiled 1983-84. Published by *Prairie States Publication*, Prophetstown, Ill. Page 22.

(21) R.M. Corbit, B.S. and LL.B, Editor-In-Chief, *History Of Jones County Past and Present. Chicago* published by S.J. Clark Publishing Co. 1910.

(22) R.M. Corbit, B.S. and LL.B, Editor-In-Chief, *History Of Jones County Past and Present. Chicago,* published by S.J. Clark Publishing Co. 1910.

(23) R.M. Corbit, B.S. and LL.B Editor-In-Chief, *History Of Jones Coun-*

ty *Past and Present, Chicago* published by S.J. Clark Publishing Company 1910.

(24) R.M. Corbit, B.S. and LL.B Editor-In-Chief, *History Of Jones County Past and Present., Chicago* published by S.J. Clark Publishing Company 1910.

(25) Corn dodgers recipe by Mrs. F.L. Gillette, Royal Publishing Company 1889. Philadelphia and Chicago.

## Chapter 5

(26) *The History Of Jones County,* 1879 Western Historical Company 1879 (reprint) in 1979 for *The Jones County Historical Society* by The Print Shop, Dixon, Illinois 1979.

(27 *The History Of Jones County,* 1879 Western Historical Company 1879 (reprint) in 1979 for *The Jones County Historical Society* by The Print Shop, Dixon, Illinois 1979.

(28) Dubuque Telegraph Herald 1928 addition (the newspaper clipping was just a scrap and the exact date of the issue was missing).

(29) Irvin Webber's material from Volume 4 – *History of Iowa City,* published for the Lions Club, 1987.

(30) Researched records of the U.S. Army, Library of Congress and the *Jones County Old Settlers Association* by William E. Corbin.

## Chapter 6

(31 *The History Of Jones County* 1879 Western Historical Company 1879 (reprint) in 1979 for the Jones County Historical Society by The Print Shop Dixon, Illinois, 1979. Page 530.

(32) *History of Johnson County, Iowa,* from 1836 to 1882. Iowa City; 1882. Pages 572-573 reprinted by Higginson Book Company, 148 Washington Street, P.O. Box 778 Salem, Massachusetts. 01970.

(33) R.M. Corbit, B.S. and LL.B, Editor-In-Chief, *History Of Jones County Past and Present. Chicago* published by S.J. Clark Publishing Company, 1910.

(34) William Wilkie, *Dubuque on the Mississippi,* Loras College Press 1987.

(35) Wikipedia article, *Panic of 1857.*

(36) *History of Johnson County, Iowa,* from 1836 to 1882. Iowa City, 1882. Pages 572-573. Reprinted by Higginson Book Company, 148 Washington Street, P.O. Box 778 Salem, Massachusetts 01970.

pages 235, 236.

(37) Taken liberally from the *Encyclopedia Dubuque*, www.encyclopedia-dubuque.org.

(38) 1880 *History of Dubuque County, Iowa*, Western Historical Company, Chicago 1880. Page 39.

(39) Len Kruse, edited by Robert Byrne. My Old Dubuque Collected Writings on Dubuque Area History Center for Dubuque History, Loras College, Dubuque, Iowa 2000.

Other books by Douglas Monk:
Heart To Heart Volume 1
Heart To Heart Volume 2

CPSIA information can be obtained
at www.ICGtesting.com
Printed in the USA
LVOW07*2204250117

522185LV00004B/6/P